THANK YOU FOR MY GREEN CARD

Edgar May

Muckross Publishing

SHIRES ❧PRESS

www.northshire.com

Thank You For My Green Card/ Edgar May. -- 1st ed.

ISBN 978-1-60571-292-5

Publisher's Notes:

This is a memoir. Names, characters, places, dates and incidents are a product of the author's memory and are identified as accurately as possible.

Posthumously edited by Madeleine May Kunin and Sarah Clay.

Copyeditors: Sarah Clay and Maria Reade.

A version of Chapter 1 was previously published in the *Vermont Sunday Magazine* of the *Rutland Herald*, June 10, 1990. It is reprinted here with permission.

For Renée May, my mother, without whose courage this book never could have been written.

TABLE OF CONTENTS

CHAPTER ONE

Coming to America

I can still hear it. The applause. Improbable applause, a tension releasing timpani of sound celebrating a rescue: *Our Rescue.*

It was the very first morning. My mother had told me and my 6-year-old sister to get dressed early. It was important to be dressed and on the ocean liner's deck on the morning we were coming to America.

The applause was hesitant at first. Tentative. Unsure if this was the right moment, if it was the right thing to do. As the statue became visible, her lighted torch poking through the mist, the sound expanded, separating into waves, spilling across the decks of the ship, carried on the chilled wind of that early June morning. The clapping was strengthened with an underpinning of cheers, hugging... grinning passengers congratulating each other in the chatter of language that sometimes neither understood, waving at the statue like school girls, with their handkerchiefs and scarves, a montage of colored streamers in the wind. The tugboats joined the rising chorus with their deep throat horn instruments punctuated by their piped whistles against the soundboard of the sea.

June 10, 1940... the decks of the USS Manhattan bonded a disparate community of strangers after eight days on sometimes angry, froth-tossed seas that eventually slipped into a gray, seamless horizon... eight days of U-boat submarine watches, warnings, imagined sightings and, always, the daily life boat drills. Nearly 2,000 of us were packed into a ship built to carry 900 passengers. Even as a young boy, counting the lifeboats and the swirl of people around them, I sensed a touch of make believe around these drills—maybe there were enough boats for the normal count of 900 passengers, but more than twice that number?

The next day's *New York Times* reported:

> The United States liner Manhattan which has evacuated more Americans from Europe than any other ship, arrived here yesterday–1,907 in all, 1,052 of them United States citizens.

> The ship also brought in refugees from Germany, Denmark, Norway, Poland and Belgium. There were children, priests, nuns, noblemen, shipping officials, students and business men aboard... cots were set up in the public rooms. Seventy-four men, most of them clergymen, slept in the Palm Court; eighty-two slept in the Grand Salon, thirteen in the gymnasium, eight in the children's playground, fifty-two in the post office on E deck, and sixty-eight in the third class lounge.

> The SS Manhattan docked at Pier 18 on the West Side of the city. That same morning Benito Mussolini announced

Italy was declaring war on the Allies, joining Germany in the devastation of Europe. Ships now were blocked in Italian ports like Genoa. The USS Manhattan had sailed from that port eight days earlier. Years later I wondered what might have been if that declaration of war had come a week sooner.

"The hand that held the dagger has struck it into the back of its neighbor," President Franklin D. Roosevelt told an anxious audience in a special national broadcast the night of our arrival. It was part of a day that included other headlines: "Nazi Tanks Now 35 miles from Paris."

It was a time of split personality, parallel lives that chronicled the normalcy of daily events against the impending rumbles of war. New York's summer theater would open with Helen Hayes appearing in "Twelfth Night" and Orson Welles in the lead in "King Lear."

The previous Sunday night the captain of the Manhattan, George V. Richardson, had ordered the ship's running lights turned off and the portholes curtained in black so as not to attract the attention of prowling German submarines. The Manhattan had left behind advancing German armies and the specter of concentration camps awaiting her Jewish passengers. It was her fifth and last pre-war voyage from Italy, evacuating Americans fleeing Europe. Among them were sixty nuns and 200 Catholic clergymen, nearly half of whom had been at the American College in Rome. This American outpost at the Vatican had become one of the first war casualties. It had closed for the first time since it opened in 1838.

Our sailing had been delayed for eighteen hours to allow the last fleeing Americans to reach the ship. With each postponement my mother became more nervous. She already had been trained in adversity. My father drowned in Lake Zurich, taking his own life. For me his suicide became a permanent festering wound, an emotional injury that would never quite heal. How could he do that! Leave me without a father!

It marooned my mother, leaving her widowed at 38, facing that extraordinary decision alone: To abandon Europe on the fringes of a war. She was driven by the universal immigrant conviction that her children would be safe and life would be better for them in America.

Some members of our family already had escaped from continental Europe, a few to England, several to America. A French cousin, living in Paris as an amateur portrait painter, was in the "underground," the French Resistance. André Brunshwieg's story of cunning and courage is among the multitude of untold, unlikely dramas of the war. After the German army occupied the city he volunteered his artistic skills to forge identity cards, and "official" documents for the Paris Underground. One morning a colleague found him at work to tell him the Gestapo knew what he was doing and were coming for him that afternoon. He immediately went home to pick up his wife. That afternoon they took the next train to his native Alsace on the French–Swiss border.

Living in a small border village, dressed in his ever-present beret and paint stained smock, every morning he carried his artist's easel and a work-in-progress canvas into the countryside, sometimes passing German border patrols. He kept a log of those encounters until he knew exactly the time the patrols arrived at a tree lined border point.

One sunny afternoon, accompanied by his wife who was carrying a picnic basket and the obligatory red checkered tablecloth, he consulted his log for the maximum time between patrols. Whoosh! Easel, canvas, beret, wife and artist scampered across into neutral Switzerland. The Swiss promptly arrested him for illegal entry and held him in the Basel city jail. Just as promptly he started painting the Basel Police Chief's portrait that would hang for many post-war years in the police headquarters. It was an artistic offering that may well have saved him and his wife. The Swiss sometimes returned the fleeing Jewish refugees to German authorities and to near certain death in the gas chambers.

Edgar with his parents, Renée and Ferdinand, 1930.

Cousin Andre's flight was not unique. Other cousins, in Holland, were saved from the death camps in similar dramas that fused intense moral values with extraordinary courage. The Dutch cousins lived a wartime experience reminiscent of the Anne Frank story, except they were hidden separately and moved from one hiding place to another. Millie, the wife (and my first cousin) and her daughter Yvonne (later, Yvonne Gibby) survived. The father, Eric Malikovsky, was caught and shipped to a concentration camp, marked by his religious faith. He was never heard from again.

Two different Christian neighbors in Amsterdam hid Millie and Yvonne in their attics sharing food rations with them, knowingly risking their lives should they have been caught harboring Jews. For security reasons, the two neighbors did not know about the other's hidden attic guest. Neither mother nor her daughter knew the other had been saved until the day the war ended.

A few of our family were not the beneficiaries of such heroics. They were herded into cattle cars bound for the human ovens of camps like Dachau. Among them was my aunt, my father's sister, Augusta May Grunewald and her husband, Sigmund. They had traveled from Germany to Holland for an emergency family meeting about leaving the danger zone.

Their three sons decided to abandon Europe immediately. Kurt and Max to Israel, Ernst to America. Augusta and Sigmund fretted about leaving their native country. It was the only place they ever had called home. They believed they were German, just like their Christian neighbors. They could not comprehend their government would kill them just because of how they worshiped God. They took the train back to Germany. After the war, captured German documents listed their names in proper alphabetical order, in the impeccable record keeping of the German killing machine

Another family member, my cousin, the son of my grandfather's brother, was a French soldier who had fought the Germans in the first days of the war. He was captured and eventually released from a prisoner of war camp without ever having his religious faith identified. He made his way back to the Mediterranean coast. A French neighbor in Nice, wanting to curry favor with the German occupiers, turned him in. He was the last male to carry the Bloch family name. His murder in a German concentration camp ended the family lineage that in the early 1800s had included a Grand Rabbi of Alsace Lorraine.

My family's historical markers are hardly unique. These stories were common, re-enacted with the repetition of a phonograph needle stuck in a scratch on a vinyl record. The same refrain again and again, sometimes reappearing years later in the sleep disrupted subconscious of those who survived. Each memory is shaded differently, a very personal marker, a flesh and blood account of the last days of a relative who was among the six million babies, children, mothers, fathers, sisters, brothers, aunts, uncles who died in the gas chambers.

"Bad things" have personal meaning, especially when they are imprinted on the growing-up-years of a young boy. After my father's sudden death, my mother sent me to live briefly with my Dutch cousins in Amsterdam. Cousin Ernst suddenly had become a stand-in for my missing father.

I particularly remember the kite. Ernst had bought me a kite kit. We assembled it together, carefully following the diagram on the instruction leaflet. We flew it on the wind-swept fields beyond the city that were like squares on a chess board, patterning the seemingly endless grid of canals. The kite was triangular, yellow and red with a flashing silver tail. It filled its paper chest, straining defiantly against the wind, swooping, diving, zooming upward in a spectacular ballet performed against a blue sky day.

Zurich, early 1930s.

Ernst also bought me a goldfish. He lived in a small angular glass aquarium that you instantly knew was the home of a goldfish. A few years later, my fish became an aquatic symbol for the impending war. When I returned to Switzerland I had to leave him in Amsterdam. And a few years later, after the German armies invaded Holland and Belgium, less than a month before our mother brought us to America, my 10-year-old imagination was sure that the German soldiers had captured my goldfish. Maybe even swallowed him whole. Or just flushed him down the toilet. I stored a mix of memories and imagination in a secret file guarded zealously by all 10-year-old boys. It was there that I kept my conjured pictures of fearsome German submarines, ranks of helmeted German soldiers on the march, and massive Swastika-marked cement bunkers facing the English Channel.

Edgar and Madeleine, 1934.

But on that June morning when we arrived in America, the war-time trauma was obscured, for my sister and me, overwhelmed as we were by the excitement of that ocean voyage and our arrival in New York. It was unlike anything we had ever experienced; sometimes it was dream-like. On the ship people were crowded into every conceivable space. Our cabin, built for four, slept nine people and a baby. The baby made an impression on everybody. It cried, lustily, every night.

Edgar and Madeleine around 1935.

I remember a night-long storm, silhouetted by a horizon-wide performance of explosive lightning whose percussion thunder was followed by the immediate reverberations of rumor. A German submarine, the gossipers said, had fired on us. A Polish refugee, a survivor of the siege of Warsaw, became hysterical. The ship's officers said it was a thunderclap, that's all. But the knowing nods of some of the older passengers tilted the deck side analysis to unseen underwater boats whose terror I would not really understand until later when I saw their menacing periscopes aimed at some of my wartime movie heroes like James Cagney, John Wayne and Cary Grant.

The dawn of our arrival, military aircraft flew overhead just before the ship's loudspeakers announced the sight of land. By then the news that Italy had entered the war spread throughout the ship. Everyone was certain the planes were there for us, the first sure sign of American protection.

By mid-morning the immigration boat had pulled alongside. It was a mini floating version of Ellis Island. The inspectors boarded the liner and worked from long tables in the dining room. My mother shepherded us through as the tugboats inched the ocean liner into the slit of the 18th Street pier. We were on deck when the gangplanks were lowered. When they touched land, amid rattling chains, another cheer blotted out all other sounds, picking up volume with an echoing chorus from hundreds of welcoming voices on the dock.

There was a sorting of the 1,907 passengers. Their social hierarchy was instantly visible by the tell-tale baggage. For the dominant group, all shapes of rough woolen bulging bags, some wicker baskets, and a scattering of scuffed suitcases held together with strands of rope. For the others, brass banded leather steamer trunks, shiny black, beribboned hat boxes, totems that separated the first class passengers.

Among the throng on shore were our cousins, Fred Kahn and his wife Irene. They had been waiting on the dock since early morning. Fred was the family's advance guard, coming from Germany 13 years earlier. He was part of the immigrant wave of the Twenties in search of adventure and opportunity. He found both. Opportunity in a $4 a week dishwashing job at a Manhattan restaurant; adventure in nightly scratching skirmishes with bedbugs whose biting furies drove him to change lodgings four times in his first four nights in America. Each time he left a week's deposit. By the June morning of our arrival, Fred had been promoted to head waiter at Broadway's Monterey restaurant and had become the family greeter of ocean liners bringing brothers, in-laws and cousins fleeing Europe. Ours was the eighth—and last—boat he met.

In many of those years Fred and Irene were a two-person Refugee Resettlement agency. By his count they welcomed "17 singles," brothers, cousins and two families. He found rooms in New York City for each of them, residential apartments for the families, paid the first week's rent and stocked each with a first bag of essential groceries.

In the crowd on the pier, Irene was the one we spotted first. She was a sartorial symphony in red—red pillbox hat, red pocketbook, red shoes and matching red gloves.

Red!

The memory is cemented into family lore. My mother would recount it through the years, still marveling at the coordinated color outfit that became the symbol of style and independence in our new land.

Fred navigated us through the bustling pier collecting suitcases and bags with the aplomb of a seasoned tour guide while Irene issued heavily German accented instructions in what I thought was perfect English. My mother spoke some fragmentary version of our new language, but my sister and I had roughly a three-word vocabulary—yes, no and bathroom.

Irene had been examining my sister and me with a critical eye from the moment we trundled down the gangplank. She focused, no, stared, at my sister's no-nonsense Swiss haircut. To duplicate it you needed only a bowl over her head and to snip off everything that showed.

"Mud-Lehn!" she commanded, "In America you gotta haff coils."

The next day, with the arrival excitement still flickering like home movie frames on my mind, I realized I *really* was in America. Wondrous, teeming, sky-scrapered America. Giant, lights-flashing, bill-boarded, neck-craning America. Here darkness was banished, replaced by 24 hours of continuous, constant, twitching, flashing electric splashes that illuminated the deep, dark canyons of streets slicing through those not-to-be-believed tall buildings. I would twist my head backward, as far as it would go, so I could see the top of those buildings, way, way up there in the sky. They just disappeared in that sky.

But it was the Automat—the food emporium—that eclipsed even the skyscrapers. The Automat introduced me to modern, chrome-trimmed, efficient America. There is was, all wrapped up in one place just a few steps from our hotel. An entire gleaming wall of what seemed like hundreds of cubicles, each with its own glass door. Behind them were more sandwiches, salads, cakes, and pies than I had ever seen. All you needed were some nickels and dimes to drop in the slots. Click, click and the door would open. Just like that. You had exactly what you saw, what you wanted. I remember staring at the empty cubicles to see what would happen next. Within minutes a flash of hands would appear with a replacement plate. *Click!* And the glass window would show another tempting offering. It was only a hand, no bodies, no faces. Just the flash of fingers. *Click.* Presto! A fresh plate. Those mysterious hands kept everything filled. Here was America. Modern, automated, shiny chromed America. The Automat became my first lesson of equality in America. Freedom in America.

In those first weeks the Automat was a warm comfort zone. It was like a child's blanket, a safe haven where I could escape the bondage of not being understood, not knowing the words, not being able to read the restaurant menu. A few clicks and the door would open, right in front of you. Freedom of choice. Escape from hesitatingly pointing your finger to tell somebody what you wanted. Relief from trying to decipher the linguistic mysteries of New York City lunch countermen: "Gimme a BLT on toast" or, "a couple sunny-side up."

No one had to speak in the Automat. Everybody was equal. A 10-year-old boy and his kid sister, fresh off the boat, were as equal as the genuine American streetcar conductor sipping his coffee at the next table. I couldn't wait for mealtimes during those first days. My pleadings were always for the Automat. It was always crowded. There were lots of different languages at the tables. But there was no need for a common one. Just the coins. I was sure, *really sure,* the Automat was invented just for immigrants. It had to be that way. Absolutely!

Years later I occasionally would pass one of the last Automats. There was a frayed garment air about them. They were patronized now by men with permanent beard stubble, hunched over a long cooled cup of coffee, bridging the gap between hustling enough coins for the next cheap wine bottle. And old women coming for some conversation, *any* conversation, while sorting through their small, worn purses for the needed coins to feed the waiting slots.

When the last of the Automats disappeared I think my immigrant era seemed to blur. But immigrant roots don't atrophy through the decades. Wonderment at opportunity in an adopted land doesn't disappear.

Some years ago I was returning from my assignment as a United States Foreign Service Officer in Paris. The jumbo jet was full. My section included a large group of students coming home from their junior year abroad. When we approached New York City the captain banked the plane over the harbor. He explained the maneuver: he wanted us to see the statue with her lighted torch reaching into the pastel blue. At the end of his announcement there was spontaneous applause, hesitant at first, then mounting throughout the cabin, augmented by student whistles and cheers.

And then, moments later, I was applauding with them.

CHAPTER TWO

Religion

Our coming to America was like a war novel whose theme was escape and rescue. For me, filtered through the prism of a 10-year-old boy, it was much more. It was often jarring, a collision of exhilaration buffeted by frustration.

It was a singular discovery of unimaginable surroundings: Food I had never tasted, new sounds and smells... most of all, a language I couldn't understand. Frustrating silences, hanging like empty spaces over my head. Like word balloons in comic strips without any writing inside the circles. They were blank, awkwardly vacant.

Simultaneously, everything was encased in a marvel of sky-scrapers that created a city of canyons—deep, narrow, shad-owed canyons—that were illuminated by never-extinguished lights. The initial wonder obscured the complete picture, tem-porarily hiding it behind the euphoria of discovery.

It was a handshake that helped me sort things out. A sim-ple handshake, an every-day, habitual greeting among strangers. It may have been only a passing snapshot in the crowded album of my life, but for me it was profound because it spoke to my personal shadows and diminished them. It altered my perception of who I was, illuminating the place where I might fit in the complex panorama of the world in front of me. That handshake began to erode my emotional self-imposed guilt, removing, slowly, very slowly, the barriers to who I might become.

It was the day Albert Einstein visited our summer camp. I had sensed it was a special day because it required a rehearsal for the entire camp. All of us, campers, counselors, the cooks, dishwashers, everybody. We needed a practice run to eliminate any possible glitches before the arrival of the famous visitor. We rehearsed lining up—over and over again—until we were about as orderly as any fidgety row of children can get.

Maybe it was because he shared the immigrant label that he made a special effort to meet each of us. *Every single one of us.* I was so smitten by this gesture that for a full week I refused to wash the hand that shook the hand of Albert Einstein. Unfortunately nothing rubbed off. A few years later I flunked Algebra.

For me that handshake always was much more than just meeting the famous. It trumped my seeing President Roosevelt in an open touring car on Forest Hills' Queens Boulevard. Bigger, even a lot bigger, than my first trip to Ebbets Field to see the Brooklyn Dodgers—my heroes—real life ballplayers, coming out of the dugout just before everybody got up to sing "The Star-Spangled Banner."

We had only a "Hello-Sir-I'm-Edgar" conversation, Albert Einstein and me.

He didn't know it, but with that handshake I was certain we had bonded, fused as accidental actors in what for me was *the* emotional drama of our time. He became a symbol of survival. He was an immigrant, just like me, in our new country. Most important, he was a publicly acknowledged immigrant. Everybody knew it! An immigrant who was Jewish. And everybody knew that too! Albert Einstein, world famous mathematician was a *Jewish refugee* who was welcomed—actually *welcomed*—in America! That really mattered to me. It was my first lesson on a long learning curve—it was okay to be Jewish, okay to be an immigrant *and* Jewish in America.

I may have been only at the dawning of my teenage years, but that was old enough to carry the baggage of the past. I knew what the Star of David meant when Hitler's laws demanded that the six-pointed symbol had to be pinned on the coat of everyone who had any Jewish blood—any Jewish blood. Even for a distant relative who long ago had abandoned his religion or who might have converted to Christianity many years earlier. I knew about our family members who were forced to wear that star before they were herded into cattle cars and transported to the "Final Solution."

It made me fearful to explain who I was, to explain all of me. It was a shadow, an internal tremor of fear—*somebody could find out.* Somebody would know that I was different: Labeled unacceptable before they even knew anything about me. *Anything.* It remains an awkward, uncomfortable smudge on my life's journey—an embarrassment, a perpetual garment of guilt. It was a personal weakness that I had dressed my religious faith in the cloth of anonymity, camouflaging it behind verbal gymnastics, dodging, twisting to avoid it.

When a conversation was about going to church on Sunday, I tried to change the subject before it got to me. My deception was assisted by my blond hair, blue eyes and that I came from a tourist celebrated Alpine nation. Swiss and Jewish? Improbable. Furthermore, my name was not an instant clue. It was not Cohen, or Schwartz. I knew no Yiddish, the language of the Ghetto streets of Eastern Europe. For me it was a foreign tongue that belonged to the Polish and Russian Jews and not to the self-proclaimed "more refined" immigrants from Western Europe.

I didn't fit among the stereotype pictures that hung in some of the contemporary museums of the mind. But the pretense, no, the denial, didn't work. It was a temporary deception that carried its own punishment. People would talk freely in front of me when they thought the target of their prejudice was nowhere in sight. They didn't suspect that the "*They*" they were talking about included me.

Forest Hills, our Plymouth Rock toe-hold in America, was a split-personality suburb of New York City. Bisected territory, sliced in two by the railroad track, but halved more firmly by the chasm separating its two cultures—one foreign, the other native. The tracks belonged to the Long Island Railroad that every morning funneled the suburbanites to their sky-scrapered Manhattan work towers.

Our half of Forest Hills was literally on the restricted side of those railroad tracks, where Jews couldn't buy houses. It sheltered an expanding tribe of immigrants, in middle class, high-rise apartment buildings that were a marvel to me. Our sixth floor, the top floor, Apartment 6E, was the highest place I had ever called home.

The playground at the end of our block was the gossip center where mothers and grandmothers not only kept an eye on the children, but dissected the latest immigrant tales. More often than not, they were spoken in the comfort of the "old country's" language. Occasionally, a mother who wanted to flaunt her progress in English-for-Adults class demonstrated her achievement in a compote of helter-skelter tenses that were periodically flavored with inventive English-accented German words.

Beyond that playground, on the other side of the railroad tracks, was Forest Hills Gardens, a trimmed lawn community of ivy-walled houses, tree-shaded streets and property deeds with specific clauses identifying the kind of people you couldn't sell your house to. The people from my side of the tracks were on that list.

There was a bridge, however. A narrow bridge, one that forced at least some integration of the two disparate communities. The bridge was called Public School 101. It was in Forest Hills Gardens, on the "right" side of the tracks. Public education's limited resources, not the bifurcated two-world cultures, dictated its location. It was the school for both halves of the divided territory.

That school was a life-changing place for me. It turned me into an out-of-the-shell-emerging embryonic American, learning new customs and, cautiously, a mysterious language called English. It was my fourth grade teacher who pulled, tugged and dragged me into the New World, one new word at a time. She would sometimes stay after school to read a few pages from a special book she had bought. Reading to me, repeating the words under the pictures, repeating them, repeating them until the marriage between picture and word was consummated, engraved in my cranium.

I have never forgotten her. More than anyone, this hairtied-in-a-bun teacher's skill and generosity helped form a pimpled immigrant into a budding, emerging word-afternew-word American. My future, joyful adventures with the English language were seeded, tended, nurtured by that fourth grade teacher.

It was not until many years later that I understood that she had a powerful helper: my mother. From the earliest days in Forest Hills there was an unbending, non-negotiable rule. Renée May might ask my sister and me a question in the old country's dialect, but we had to answer in English. Always in English. If we were tempted to take a shortcut in Swiss, she pretended she didn't hear us. The uncomfortable silence reinforced the rule without the need of an explanation.

Our mother understood that if her children were going to be "real Americans" there could be no room for conversations flecked with even a hint of the tell-tale foreign accent, the instant identity marker of the immigrant community around us. "Only English Spoken Here" was an uncompromising command. It was like a constant flashing billboard anchored in every room. It was an imperative so we would both become indistinguishable from those around us, not separate, not different, but an indistinguishable part of many.

But even the juggernaut team of my fourth grade teacher and my mother couldn't entirely bridge the gap of our two worlds. Even with my new words, I knew I was different. Sometimes, awkwardly separate—not quite equal. It was inscribed in the details of daily living.

One of my new friends who lived in Forest Hills Gardens asked me to join his Boy Scout troop. The troop was sponsored by the congregation of an ivy-covered, gothic-designed church. Even though I spoke "funny," I was welcomed. Those first few weeks produced the bonding that has no barriers among the young. Until... until I was asked if I wanted to come to church next Sunday. It was a simple question. It required a simple answer. There was no wiggle room. No adroit maneuver.

"Thank you," I said, wondering if the taut expression on my face already told them. "I don't think so," I paused. "I'm Jewish."

There was no immediate response, only a nod. The next week the Scoutmaster asked to see me in his cubicle of an office. Even at 11 years of age I recognized a conversation that neither party wanted to have. It was adorned in the diplomatic niceties that are meant to soften reality. "We're really a Scout Troop for this neighborhood," he said. "We've never had any boy from the *other part of Forest Hills*." The distillation was uncomplicated. I was asked to leave.

The following year the "not quite equal" shadow appeared again. My mother had listened to a cousin's wartime paranoia. He warned her about a possible German submarine shelling of the City or a bombing of New York. She decided that we needed to move to the safety of a smaller community and found a house in upstate New York in a quiet, genteel neighborhood. My mother was about to sign the sales contract when the realtor cautiously brought up the subject.

"You said you were Swiss? Right?"

"Yes," she answered, "I was born there."

"Good, very good," was the exhaled response, "... beautiful country. One day I'd like to see those mountains," he said in the preamble to *the* question, "I hope you don't mind my asking. They're just formalities... there are some covenants... in the deed to the house."

My mother nodded without the slightest idea what the word "covenant" meant in her new, adopted language.

"You'll want to go to church in the neighborhood, I suppose?"

She answered without emotional adornments. There was a noticeable pause. An awkward quiet space.

"I'm sorry," he said. "There are restrictive covenants... *They* don't allow me to sell... ".

But the most discomforting incident occurred later at my first full-time job. I was working during the day as a file clerk for *The New York Times.* In the evening I was enrolled in night school at Columbia University. A co-worker and I had formed a friendship that was built significantly on our daily partnership trying to outwit our usually scowling supervisor. This challenge became the verbal appetizer to our frequently shared brown bag lunch.

It turned out he was an unreconstructed model of prejudice. Almost daily, he railed against "Yids," "Kikes" and any other slur he could find for Jews. On one particularly day, after an expanded vituperative assault, my determined effort to camouflage my faith finally failed me.

"Jimmy," I said, "What is it that you have against Jews?"

"Listen," he said, "If you can show me one good Jew, I'd change my mind."

Edgar and Madeleine at a Passover dinner.

Our eyes locked. There was a space, a near frozen moment before I extended my hand nearly touching his chest. He looked at my hand. Stared at it. I saw a draining whiteness in his face. Then his eyes focused on mine. There was no conversation. He shook his head and then turned away.

These are incidents familiar to serial waves of immigrants. Those kinds of inflammatory words bond a diverse community of strangers, entwining them with the common thread that said they were different. Not quite equal to those who already were there. It is not a subtle message.

In Boston, the "Help Wanted" signs sometimes said: "Irish Need Not Apply." In Buffalo, its East side was called Polack town, where the everyday street language was more often Polish, rather than heavily accented English. The Eastern European footprint was so large in Buffalo the immigrant enclave had its own daily Polish newspaper, the largest outside of Warsaw.

In Chicago, uniformed doormen screened those who rang the entry bell of the brass knobbed, polished oak entrances of the emporiums of the affluent. Often they were exclusive social clubs where neither Catholics nor Jews were invited as members.

Even in rural America, a miniature place like my Vermont hometown, the newest immigrants from Poland had been imported to work as rag pickers in the shoddy mill. They were segregated in cheek-by-jowl houses on the bottom of the hillsides on the narrowest street in town.

The word "exclusive" sometimes was a euphemism for "restricted" creating islands of self-proclaimed superiority. They sometimes included entire neighborhoods where the price of houses was accompanied by legal restrictions that kept the new immigrants from becoming neighbors. There were new Jewish country clubs because the established ones didn't let them in. There were corporations that didn't hire Jews, or seriously limited their numbers. The leading universities had unwritten Admissions Office covenants of their own, called quotas—sometimes 5 percent, occasionally a few more. There were limits, clearly prescribed limits to the inscription on that welcoming statue in New York harbor: "Give me your tired, your poor, your huddled masses yearning to breathe free... "

In the entertainment business, sometimes heavily populated by Jews in contrast to their percentage in the population, there was a flurry of new, homogenized, Americanized names. Innocuous, unrevealing, "Made-in-America" names. Tony Curtis lived his early years as Bernard Schwartz, in the back of his father's tailor shop on New York's East side. Edward G. Robinson was rechristened, so to speak, by a Hollywood agent convinced he couldn't negotiate a movie contract for somebody named Emanuel Goldenberg. The newly minted Robinson was 10 years old, exactly like me, when his parents brought him from Romania in 1903. Then there was Benjamin Kubelesky, who emigrated from Poland with his parents, Meyer and Emma Sachs. Their son was better known after he was renamed Jack Benny.

Edgar in the Synagogue with Jane Kunin, about 2010.

Religion has been no small matter in the political syllabus of America. More often than not, it is defined by exclusion. The barrier of being different permeated high political office.

Tradition, rooted in plain reality, dictated that some political leadership roles were out of bounds for some Americans.

John Fitzgerald Kennedy is among the prominent who helped dismantle the barricade. But he succeeded only after Al Smith, the first Catholic Presidential candidate, was firmly rebuffed in 1928—in large part because of his Roman Catholic faith. It was an electoral landslide. At the end of election night Herbert Hoover had 444 Electoral College votes, Alfred P. Smith: 87.

The fear mongers had warned the Pope would come to America to instruct the President. Political folklore recorded that after the last votes were counted, Al Smith sent a one word telegram to the Pope:

"Unpack," it said.

On a few occasions the immigrant and religious handicap was muted on the very first day in America, reconstructed and Americanized in the first hour. A prominent Rochester lawyer relished telling me the story of how his last name was born on the first day his father arrived in America. He landed at Ellis Island carrying a scuffed suitcase and his birth certificate. The carefully folded document said its owner was Kashikonovsky. The Ellis Island immigration official stared at the name and shook his head without even a fly-by pronunciation effort.

"You can't have a name like that in America—I'm going to give you a good old American name," he said, filling out the required form. "From now on your name is Goldman."

Immigrant or fourth generation native, we are a tribal people. We find warmth and strength when we expand from the singular to the plural. The more plurals the better. Building a community, tentatively at first, starting in one city block of common neighbors, expanding into a new neighborhood, fastened together by the familiar. Built on a shared language, food our parents made, generation-inherited customs, and the "old country" ways of doing things wherever that old country might be. Our Forest Hills neighborhood, on the immigrant side of the railroad tracks, was one of them, but there were many other similar refugee islands newly clustered in the cities of America.

My mother used to take us to Manhattan's East Side neighborhood of Yorkville, to the Café Geiger, where the scene was only a nickel subway ride back to the comfort of the old country. There, we were warmed by a constant flow of dishes from the kitchen that mixed nostalgia with hand-written, hand-me-down recipes, whose ingredients were measured carefully, not in ounces, but in European grams. Puff pastries with vanilla cream filling, hot chocolate topped with a generous dollop of whipped cream, and Viennese Sacher torte, served by black skirted, white-aproned waitresses, and tuxedoed waiters. They took your order, in German of course, as naturally as if they were scurrying among tables on the Bahnhofstrasse at Sprüngli's, a fashionable Zurich café.

The "old country" ways became, for me, less about the past and more about the barely perceptible changes that began eroding immigrant barriers. The "not quite equal" markings gradually were fading, receding, like pages of a newspaper yellowing in their tucked away corner of the attic. The Café Geiger itself closed, shuttered long ago. The children of immigrants no longer came. We wanted to be something else—plain, vanilla Americans.

For me this was more than just another change in a war-fanned, smoldering world. It was profound and personal, an emotional crest that confirmed that my new country was different. It was different because of a basic American strength. Its ability to change—change that sometimes came too slowly, but change that narrowed the gap between what was real and what was written in the inscriptions engraved on our statues of patriotism.

I suspect that my grand-nephews—three generations removed from my immigrant label—reading about these signposts of my life might conclude that I made them up. They have no framework of experience to confirm them. Anymore than—for the first time ever, after the election of Barack Obama—telling a black child that when she or he grows up they can't be President of the United States.

Understanding this capacity for change was exhilarating, emotional for me, something like opening a birthday present and finding exactly what you had wished for. I particularly remember one of those presents. It happened in my first newspaper job in Vermont. I was covering the funeral of the first Vermont soldier killed in the Korean War.

His name was Sgt. Reuben Miller, and he died on a Korean hillside June 14, 1952. His funeral was a state-wide event because there is a fascination about "the firsts" of our human journeys, even if that first is about death, the death of a young Vermonter. For me it was more than that, a landmark more. Because Reuben Miller was Jewish.

He was a member of one of three Jewish families in a call-me-by-my-first-name town where everybody knew everybody. Not to mention each other's business, aided substantially by four-party telephone lines that allowed multiple listeners to eavesdrop on conversations, theoretically, between two people.

The funeral contradicted the stereotypes. Like a searchlight beam slicing through a black sky, it illuminated our ability to change, without fanfare, without drama. Bellows Falls (pop. 3,906) shut down on the morning of Reuben Miller's funeral. There were handmade signs in the store windows. Crayon-on-cardboard signs: "Closed until Noon for Reuben Miller's Funeral."

There were the flashing blue lights of the police cruisers, escorts for the final journey of Sgt. Reuben Miller. There was a line of cars whose end was not in sight from my sidewalk vantage point. The cruisers led the hearse on the 12 mile trip to Meyer David cemetery in Claremont, N.H., the closest Jewish burial ground. They said it was the largest funeral cortege that anyone could remember.

Amid the personal emotions rooted in my shared religious faith with that soldier, I missed the over-arching message of Sgt. Reuben Miller's funeral. Religion was far from its centerpiece. It may not even have had a walk-on part. Later—many years later—I more clearly understood that the funeral was a defining tableau of change. Fundamental American change. That long line of cars. The uniformed police in their twitching orbit of blue-lighted cruisers leading the hearse to the cemetery, past stores with their hand-lettered "Closed" signs, past lines of people with their hands over their hearts as the flag-draped coffin passed them. A New England quilt of images, colors, wind-swept flags, respectful silences, it was a montage of Americana that simply said that Sgt. Reuben Miller's neighbors had joined to bury one of their own.

CHAPTER THREE

Farm

That funeral was a seminal lesson, one of the most important in my life. It helped suture the emotional wound of my complex about my faith. It was like a long-ago scar that gradually faded into a hazy memory intruding itself only occasionally on my life. It became a milestone of change, a personal turning point, like that handshake with Albert Einstein. These were accompanied by a parallel lesson: My years on the farm, where I learned about work, plain, physical work, sometimes sweat-in-the-eyes stinging work. I learned about my place in the world around me, where nature would assert her supremacy with blunt messages—a sudden downpour that drenched acres of drying hay or a hail storm that devastated a field of wheat about to be harvested.

Just days after World War II ended, after the dancing in the streets, the hugging among strangers, confetti snow-storming from the upper windows, my mother called a family meeting. She told us that she had to go back to Switzerland to settle the unfinished business that remained in the wake of our hasty departure. My 10-year-old sister would go with her. But what to do with me?

There may have been a brief pause. It was measurable in milliseconds.

"The farm! I want to stay on our summer camp farm."

The farm was in Spellman, New Jersey, and in the mid-thirties it had become an immigrant beachhead for two Kaufman brothers and a cousin, all refugees from Hitler's Germany. They had combined their modest resources with bank loans to buy the farm at a discounted depression-era price. The venture was buttressed with a timely necessity: a summer camp partnership with our New York City immigrant congregation. The city/country alliance brought needed dollars to the struggling farm in exchange for a rural curriculum that was completely foreign to the congregation's city youngsters.

The brothers, Otto and Ernest, and their wives were farmers in the old country. There was no need for on-the-job training. They brought their farming skills with them. Like many immigrants before them, that special imported talent impressed their more rooted American neighbors. Those skills more than impressed this city boy from the very first day I arrived at the farm camp.

There it was! A farm menagerie in whose proximity I had never been. Cows, a goat, chickens, calves, geese, ducks, turkeys—a collection of Noah's Ark passengers right there in front of me. Amazing to this 14-year-old!

During that first camp week I volunteered for every farm chore. Any chore. Feeding chickens, cleaning stalls, turning hay by hand in the long rows of the fields beyond the barn. I was convinced I had found my calling, positive I was going to be a farmer. No doubt about it! I had tapped a rural reservoir in my psyche. It resonated to the vastness of the sky, the smell of new mown hay, the sight of a tottering calf born in the field a few hours earlier.

It was not until several years later that I began to understand that the marvels of nature and the rhythms of the seasons also contained the incessant drum beat of a farm's daily demands. Cows, it appeared, had no concept of weekends. They had to be milked twice a day. Every day. Chickens needed fresh grain and water daily. The only time clock on a farm was in the sky, recording the start of the day with the emerging rose-tinted dawn and ending with the layered paint strokes of a sunset.

Sen. May visiting a farm in 1984.

The negotiations between my mother and the Kaufmans were settled rapidly. The compact detailed my conversion from summer camp enthusiast to year-round eager farm assistant. I would work for my room and board, before and after school, including weekends. Unknown to me, the arrangement also included a monthly stipend from my mother, a modest lubricant that helped smooth the transfer of a city teenager with newly discovered hormones to a new life in the country. It turned out to be a fair deal. Maybe more positive for me, more than even my expansive imagination would envision.

My new farm life filled a constant, nagging void that seemed like a deep chasm—the death of my father when I was 6 years old. I never discussed those feelings with my mother. It would have been painful, awkward. Feelings that were suppressed, sometimes by gender barriers, long established tribal rituals that surfaced even in conversations of a boy with his mother. All I knew is that I had some vague perception that I had to take on the role of "the man" in the family, become an ersatz stand-in, even though I really didn't know what that meant. And I missed him, terribly. Sometimes every day. When other neighborhood boys spoke of their fathers, I didn't know what to say, what facial expression was suitable? Even the practiced slouch of a teenager became awkward, uncomfortable.

All I knew I missed him only like a boy whose father simply didn't exist. It was the farm that helped narrow, if not completely fill, that chasm. Ernest, the older brother, and his wife were childless, presenting an opportunity, like a tumble of that small steel ball skittering around the roulette wheel of life. We never talked about it. That they treated me like a son seemed not to need words. It hovered between us, like low hanging fruit for the taking.

I listened to Ernest more closely than to other adults, intent on absorbing the farm lessons I knew he also had learned as a boy. His occasional reprimands were painful because I knew I had disappointed him. It was like that. There was an unspoken, vague connection that nurtured a new warm feeling of belonging, something valuable that had been missing in my younger years.

On the more pragmatic side, farm lessons are not complicated. You either do it the right way or you don't. Add to this a teaching formula supplemented with Germanic emphasis and the instruction is even more easily understood.

Edgar and David Jarvie at Muckross, in Springfield, moving logs, 1990.

Otto, the younger of the two brothers, taught me how to drive a tractor, and how to plow a field into freshly turned dark soil that created a painting of gently curving rows whose distant furrows seemed to be swallowed by the horizon. He stood on the tractor's draw bar, gesticulating, explaining that I had to keep an eye on both the three-bladed plow behind me and, simultaneously, watch where I was going. It was a swivel-headed maneuver that seemed a real contradiction to me.

Moving firewood at Muckross, 2007.

It was. I messed up. But the introductory chapter of "Field Plowing" contained a provision for error—the first time. Maybe the second. There was a nod from my instructor that bordered on what I thought was just a trace of disappointment. The lesson was repeated; again, no passing grade. I knew the rules. Two failed tries and there are consequences—clear, un-ambiguous consequences. These came from a worn, old school rule book that contained a time tested dictum, "Spare the rod, spoil... "

"Poom, Poom!" The flat of the hand landed on the back of my neck. On the next try, apparently, I produced a near perfect furrow the length of the field. I still relish the response to this modest achievement: soft pats on my shoulder

Those farm years were like a long running play. They were repetitive. Their beginning was always identical. Every performance featured the same actors, the same scenery. Even the background sounds accompanying the dialogue were constant. Every day's curtain-raising began with the sound of footfalls in the farmhouse hallway. The groans of the worn boards warned of the impending morning call—thump after thump— preceded by the rooster's confident welcome to the dawn.

"Get up! It's time for the barn."

The voice was neither threatening nor sympathetic. It was matter-of-fact, a daily monotone without emotional adorn-ment, a ritual where both speaker and reluctant listener rec-ognized the inevitability of having to abandon a warm bed. In its repetitive certainty, it reflected the inner working that is the ticking pulse of daily and seasonal rhythms of farm life. The farm was a place where my important lessons did not come from a book, but came wrapped in the swirl of nature around me. These were certain, the comforting signposts of the seasons.

They began with the stirrings of the land in spring time, the first tender shoots of the fall-planted rye reaching for the warming sun. The rebirth of the land that feeds us. And, the crucial, repeated lesson that humankind is not at the center of the universe. Confirmation that mortals must bow to the larger realities around us—the powerful moods of nature, periodic temper tantrums exploding in the sky, carried by the bellowing wind, the slanting rain. They shaped the message that each day's farm agenda is ruled by unseen hands that manipulate events in the sky.

For boys exposed to this rural cycle, words like "warm" and "cold" have a different meaning than the dispassionate, matter-of-fact urban vocabulary that appears in digital temperature markings on the living room thermostat.

"Warm" on the farm sometimes registered in sweat, mixed with alfalfa dust, stinging in every open pore as I rolled hay in the summer heat of a 100 plus degree haymow.

"Cold" was the I-can't-help-it teeth chattering as I carried full milk pails from the warm barn to the frost-shrouded milk house, 50 feet away. These were lessons that affirmed that weather is the ultimate arbiter of country life, a truth that surfaced each dawn, beginning with those footfalls on creaking farmhouse floorboards.

My bedroom had no heat. A few wisps of warmth from the wood stove in the kitchen below managed to slip through the dried cracks between the floorboards. Winter asserted itself with an exhaled frosty cloud, like the word balloons in the comic books I secretly read under the covers within the orbit of my flashlight's narrow circle. Each morning the twisted sculpture of the washcloth clung to the towel rack, as stiff as a partially uncovered corpse in a windswept field after a blizzard. It confirmed the cold just in case you needed any validation.

The chill of the room accentuated the warmth of my body filling the cocoon of my feather bed and its companion of blankets. It was a nightly return to the beginning; to the predawn of my life, a nocturnal fetal floating tranquility.

Sugaring with nephews Adam and Daniel Kunin.

Every morning I grabbed my underwear from an adjacent chair and put them on underneath the covers, in a twisting shimmying, contorted dance. It was the most pragmatic farm maneuver I ever learned, that reluctant exit from bed. The sequel was not more comforting. The "dress code" for farm workers at the time was as standard as army fatigues—denim overalls complete with shoulder straps hitched to brass buttons, wool cap, and green rubber boots speckled with flecks of manure that the barn hose didn't wash off the previous evening.

Fishing at Muckross, 1980s.

Because my rural uniform tended to absorb and shelter the aromatic scents of the cow barn, the farm wives banned the overalls from the house, exiling them to an abandoned outhouse next door. On many a winter morning the overalls waited for me, standing upright like frozen sentinels. All I needed to do was step into them and march stiff-legged to the barn.

Snowshoeing on Muckross Pond, with Peter, Lisa and Will Kunin, 1995.

My rural curriculum had been launched with a simple conversation between our rabbi and my mother. I later learned their assessment was based on something more than the contemporary child-rearing orthodoxy that summer camp was an idyllic respite for a child from the city. Both my mother and the rabbi were convinced that for me especially, farm life would provide preventive and therapeutic insurance to cover just-in-case future troubles, due to my growing up without a father. It was a clairvoyant evaluation.

Rabbi Hugo Hahn, like most of his flock, also was a refugee from Hitler's hate. As he had in the old country, he delivered his Saturday morning sermons in German, fortified by the clipped Teutonic cadence that instantly produced rabbinical gravitas. No one, gray-haired adult or peach-fuzzed youngster, dared address him other than "Herr Doktor Rabbi Hahn." In my case, since I clearly needed any additional good grace I could locate, the salutation was embellished with a modest bow.

In his long flowing black robes, the tall, hefty delegate of God towered over his youngest congregants like me, solemnly pronouncing—very solemnly—the biblical verities that must be drilled into the head of every young boy to redirect any potential less than noble instincts.

Like so many of his calling, the rabbi had that extraterrestrial skill that allowed him to identify boys who were going to be trouble—trouble before they opened their first prayer book on the time-honored path to Jewish manhood, the bar mitzvah. There was hardly a lesson where I failed to confirm the rabbi's instincts. I don't remember which was more fearsome, the incomprehensible Hebrew text or the not-so-well-disguised pain on Herr Doktor Rabbi Hahn's face as I mangled the words of both the Torah reading and the obligatory introductory prayers. Thankfully, the rabbi had an emergency solution for these discomforting occasions—a crisis-induced short cut.

I was convinced both the rabbi and God himself had come to my rescue. A few Saturday mornings later I stood at the altar in front of the whole congregation—*the whole congregation*—repeating my oft rehearsed, abbreviated presentation. It was the first and only time I ever heard my own heart pound.

The rabbi had a slight smile on his face as he handed me the congregation's inscribed Bible to mark the occasion. The rabbinical expression, I always suspected, was an exhaling sigh of relief that he managed to pull me over this barrier and safely out of his weekly confirmation class. My mother, on the other hand—as mothers are so inclined—was beaming, proud as if I had just won a gold medal in the Bar Mitzvah Olympics.

In the critical index of a life's journey, these personal memories are as indelible and enduring as that first sighting of the statue of freedom in New York harbor. They are more than a recounting. My farm years blended the every-day routine with the larger mysteries confronting humankind. Those years brought me perspective in the sometimes perplexing world around me. The accumulated chapters of knowledge included more than the mechanics of farming, more than the miracle of the change of seasons.

One experience involved Mr. Harrison. He was a tall, never stoop-shouldered man who had one overwhelming characteristic you couldn't miss: he was black. The sculptured grooves in his face and his calloused hands told of age and a life of manual labor. He and his family were down-the-road neighbors. Mr. Harrison occasionally worked on the farm, cutting lawn around the house, helping repair machinery, repainting the seemingly endless supply of flaking whitewash peeling from barn walls. On many days we did chores together.

From the very first introduction all of us were firmly told to call him "*Mister Harrison.*" It was so thoroughly drilled into us that I now can't remember if I ever knew his first name. Only years later did I understand that this contained a much larger message. There was an unspoken thread that tied Mr. Harrison, branded by his color, to his immigrant employer who had escaped the German death camps, branded by his religion.

I knew that Mr. Harrison in some of his adult years responded to a different name. Others had called him "Boy." But I didn't have to go to my school books to learn the differences between Mr. Harrison and me. That part, somehow, had slipped from historical yesterdays into the present. The nearest movie theater to the farm was in the adjacent town of Hopewell. The theater had a special section for black people—the balcony. If they wanted to see a movie, the balcony was the place for them. The only place. Yes, in the late 1940s, in New Jersey. Fifty or so miles from New York City.

It was years later that I understood the real meaning of that balcony. I understood that if the Germans had invaded Switzerland at the beginning of the war, my mother would have been barred from bringing us to America. I would have been forced to wear a yellow six-pointed star pinned to my jacket—like all Jews, children and adults—within the German orbit of conquest.

I became aware that Mr. Harrison's movie balcony and my potential yellow star were connected. They were telling everybody that we both were different, an instant twinning, fused together by the markers of our inequality.

The lessons of youth don't disappear from life's pages. My years on the farm were a blend of the profound and the ordinary that illuminated the path from youth to adulthood. Formal school was part of it. But in retrospect, a lesser part.

My two separate paths of learning were bridged by the span connecting the rural and the academic. It was traveled every weekday. It began with the early morning hours in the barn, returning to the house to wash up, have breakfast, and change into the formal go-to-school clothes that never seemed to fit quite as comfortably as the overalls. Then the usual rush for the school bus at the end of our farm road.

The big yellow school bus turned out to be a symbol of my divided high school world. Those of us on the bus knew we were different. We had different life experiences and different priorities—after school work requirements. Like the disparities between two separate countries, we were fastened to each other only by a shared border.

The suburban and rural divide was as clear as the departure time of the yellow bus, 10 minutes after the end-of-class bell sounded. Ten minutes, promptly. The second half of the day's agenda was waiting—cows had to be milked, chickens fed. That metronome of farm rhythm was heard even above the din of teenage babble on that bus.

There was one universally recognized blockade in the country-city divide. For growing boys—and I suspect, girls—such moments are fused in life's lexicon, as firmly as the trepidation of handing over a not so stellar report card, or the memory of a long ago rabbinical reprimand, or the consequences of "third try" failure in agricultural studies. It was summarized in a single word: wheels!

The need for a simple answer to the I'm-on-the-farm and she's-in-town dilemma. The answer? A 1939 Ford two-door sedan! Black. Sleek-looking, at least to me. Newly washed, before every date. Although I didn't really understand it at the time, the fact was that the Ford presented its own country–city predicament.

I never could comprehend why when I picked up an in-town date, the first thing she would do was roll down the window, every time. Even in December, in January. Every single date, with every in-town girl! It was only many years later, at a 25th anniversary class reunion, that I finally learned from one of my former classmates turned proper matron, that the open window exercise was a self-defense mechanism. It seemed that 1939 Ford had picked up the scent of its cow barn surroundings. I was oblivious to that special aroma because my whole world smelled that way. Perfumed or not, however, I clearly understood that a car was the lynchpin to romance. It was one of two essentials in my early pursuits of a young man's fancy. The other was a 12-foot ladder.

In order to hold on to the car privilege, I had to meet the curfew. In order meet the curfew I needed the ladder. The ladder had to lean against the side of the house so I could clamber through the window of my second floor bedroom, avoiding the creaking, alarm-sounding stairway whenever I was just a tad (or a bit more) beyond the curfew.

It was my first delusional proof that male passion, even in its earliest awakenings, sweeps aside caution and common sense. I actually believed the Kaufmans didn't notice, even when the ladder reappeared every Saturday night. It just showed up at the side of the house, and somehow I thought they missed it.

I thought they didn't hear the geese either, though their squawking chorus could not be muted. The geese had free run of the farmyard, and at night they would roost in one of the sheds. It was uncanny how they would respond to the sound of the returning car; how they would follow me as I tip-toed to the ladder against the house, serenading me with their incessant chorus of welcome.

The geese, the creaking stairway, that first lesson of plowing a field, are part of the myriad panels in my collage of country life. They are as vivid today as when they first appeared on the life canvas of a boy growing up on a farm. Each with its own lesson...

...Walking my trap line before school along the ice-covered brook, and the sudden adrenaline rush of seeing the steel jaws clamped on the foot of a muskrat before it drowned; and my internal quandary, forced to balance an animal's pain versus the worth of a $4 pelt.

...Lessons from Queenie, the calf I was given to raise. The bonding between a boy and his calf, and a 4-H club project that got all tangled up in the emotional yarn of the heart. I have never forgotten that morning they loaded Queenie into the slaughterhouse truck. I just stood there. Watching her resisting, planting her hoofs in the dirt as they pulled the rope to force her into that truck. She left pitted impressions in the dirt that were deeper on one side than the other—a sculpture of resistance. I saw the hoof marks the next morning, and then the next... until they disappeared, obliterated by a cloud burst from a summer thunder storm.

It is all too easy to package growing up on a farm in the velvet wrappings of selective memory. To mute or overlook the sharper edges of a hail storm, the sweat stinging eyes in a 100 degree hayloft, the unease caused by a muskrat in a steel-jawed trap, the emotional turmoil swirling around the departure of the calf you raised.

Gardening at Muckross, 1984.

The mandatory, repetitive reality of farm life. Every day of every week of every month. The farm years taught me about work. Plain hard work. That repetitive tyranny of physical labor whether in a sun-blistered field turning rows of hay or the factory workplace where the machine's lever must be pulled every 20 seconds, in syncopated rhythm with the click-ing-clack of the assembly line. It is a shared, repetitive bore-dom that for many is welded permanently into the work day of manual labor that supports a family. Those years of country life taught me about the differences among us. The disparities. The lesson I learned from a tall co-worker called Mr. Harrison.

Working at Muckross with David Jarvie, around 1990.

These are the flashbacks of very personal feelings. They are individually nuanced, formed and filtered through the prism of my own voyage to manhood. The farm years were the most compelling education I ever received—more significant than the book learning in high school, more relevant than the teachings of my professors at the university.

Somehow I don't remember my last day on the farm. I can recall the preceding days, particularly the graduation. The celebratory smile on the face of Ernest—my home schooling professor of agricultural studies—when the principal handed me my diploma. The cheering, the flurry of mortar boards sailing in the wind like a wave of migrating birds. Classmates hugging their good-byes on the launching pad to their adulthood.

But that last day on the farm? It's a blur. A confusion of contradictory emotions. Like sorting through a stack of out of focus photographs.

Maybe I just don't want to remember that day.

Tending a Muckross flower bed, 2005.

CHAPTER FOUR

Journalism

66 **I**f you're going to write an obituary like that, you might want to consider going back to creative writing," the professor told me.

It was my first toe-in-the-water in journalism, an abrupt, jarring immersion without a life preserver in sight. It happened in the first hour of the first night of my first journalism class, just a few months after my rural education had ended and I had returned to the hurly-burly of urban congestion.

The voice belonged to John Hohenberg, a Columbia School of Journalism professor who taught an introductory night course to working adults. He began the class with an assignment to write an obituary, reciting the noteworthy biographical snippets of the departed, a 78-year-old woman who had lived in Patchogue, Long Island. Her life's journey was notable because of her prize-winning cherry pies. Since that night I have never eaten a piece of cherry pie without a shimmering image of my less-than-applauded entrance into journalism.

The professor read several of the offerings aloud and handed the rest back as the class ended. He remembered me because just before the class started, I had asked him if he thought this journalism course would harm my creative writing style, a question that only a full-of-himself 19-year-old hope-to-be-writer could frame. It was a personally constructed monument of self-importance that effortlessly finds a home among the young. The professor, long schooled in managing emerging fragile, journalistic egos, replied, without smirk or emotion, "I really don't think so."

John Hohenberg was more than a passing bit player in my newspaper career. He would show up again years later. But from the first opening obituary crisis to the end of the course, I apparently negotiated my journey to redemption. He altered his opening night assessment. Get a job on a newspaper, he said. You're ready.

I wrote to 40 New England newspapers, where resumes like mine accumulate like snowflakes in a January blizzard. Four actually answered. Three thanked me for offering myself, but said they had no openings. The fourth was from Burlington, Vermont. It included an invitation to come for an interview.

It was a long bus ride from New York City to Vermont, a short walk to the office of the *Burlington Free Press* and an even shorter interview. Maybe one of the shortest in the annals of the unemployed.

"Thanks for coming up. Where have you worked?" asked the editor.

"Well, I covered New York City Night Court... for my Columbia Journalism class," I answered, with special emphasis on the word "covered."

"No, I mean, what newspaper jobs?"

Ahhh... That long—very, very long—moment of silence that roosts in the shadows of certain conversations: with a girl you're trying to impress; with a mother who caught you at a multiple choice infraction; with a prospective employer whose face suddenly freezes into indifference.

"I'm sorry. We must have misread your resume. We're looking for somebody with experience to cover the legislature. I'm really sorry."

That is a near verbatim repetition of that entire job interview. It was back to the bus station, with more than enough time to marinate myself in the juices of rejection while waiting for the next south-bound bus.

In those days buses made periodic pit stops, acknowledging human need and the pragmatism that there was no bathroom on the bus. One of those moments of necessity was in Rutland. I remembered that my journalism professor, in one of his not infrequent class digressions, mentioned that he had a friend who was the city editor of the *Rutland Herald*. From the bus station I made the phone call: No, the city editor had moved on. No, they had no openings. But... there was a weekly in southeastern Vermont looking for a reporter.

That conversation turned into my first newspaper job, at the *Bellows Falls Times*. It paid one dollar an hour. Yes, one dollar. During my first week I was informed, by the way, that my journalistic duties included getting up at 5 a.m. every Thursday to show up in the pressroom to help assemble the eight page sections that made up the advertising-rich weekly. The repetitive, reflex motion of sections mating—slap, pause, slap, pause, slap—was the pre-dawn rhythm of my baptism in journalism. I could do it today, as I did then, half asleep.

It was the best job I ever had. I was learning by doing. My chores included the bedrock of weekly journalism: writing the personals column. *"John and Alice Stimson of Henry Street spent the weekend in Boston visiting their daughter, Allison, a sophomore at..."*

Every reader survey showed these were the best read parts of the paper. Every week was a movie reel of adventure. Multi-alarm fires, a prison break that ended in murder, a few high profile arrests and, of course, obituaries. Again it was an obituary that remains among the prominent, indelible memories. I seemed to have developed a bizarre tendency of tripping over the inert remains of those who recently left.

It was just before the Thursday deadline. For several days I had tried numerous times to reach Father Wawer, the local priest of the Polish Catholic Church, one of two in town. I needed the time of the departed's final ceremony. Each phone call brought me to his housekeeper. On that last one, distracted by the looming deadline, I absentmindedly blurted out, "Who's this? Mrs. Wawer?" There was no space between the emphatic "No" and the click of the phone returning to its cradle. I was momentarily startled by the abrupt ending until I suddenly realized that a neophyte, dollar-an-hour reporter had just tried to wipe out nearly two thousand years of priestly celibacy.

In spite of my obituary fumbles, the New England Weekly Press Association had offered some encouragement. At its annual dinner, I received several journalism prizes for feature and news articles. The *Bellows Falls Times* itself was named the Best Weekly in New England. The editor of a Massachusetts daily heard about the awards and called me with a job offer.

The young reporter.

The *Fitchburg Sentinel* was a family-owned daily in a mill town whose past glittered more brightly than its frayed, vacant-factory present. Its cramped news room was a soundboard for the tap, tap, tapping typewriters underneath a roof that required sudden, strategic shifts of man and machine to avoid the drip, drip, drip of leaks during heavy rain storms. The half dozen denizens of this enclave seamlessly blended into characters of Ben Hecht's play, *The Front Page*, with a supporting cast of street-wise refugees from a Damon Runyon tale.

One of those characters was a short, hunch-backed sports editor whose daily newsroom chores were a prelude of economic necessity, so he could tend to his nocturnal passion: boxing. He scouted, trained and paired against each other a sweaty collection of muscled toughs from the old factory towns of central Massachusetts. He introduced me to these pugilistic dramas by dragging me to a dusty prizefighting ring hidden in the paint-peeling back neighborhoods.

My education in the Manly Arts ended abruptly one night when his star pugilist turned into a still life portrait, a flat-on-the-canvas form who had been touted only hours earlier as his most prominent prospect.

His wake was conducted in a back alley tavern known to close promptly for the nightly legal curfew and, more famously, to reopen, just as promptly via a back door for those connoisseurs who wished to continue their alcoholic outing until dawn.

All I remember about that evening was waking early the next morning in what would generously be described as a modest hotel room in a challenged neighborhood. Next to me was the fully dressed, open mouthed, snoring form of the hunch-backed sports editor. I concluded right then that I needed to hitch my athletic fandom to a different spectator sport.

My tenure at the *Sentinel* was nearly as brief as my truncated introduction to boxing. Nine months after I arrived, a letter in my mailbox announced: "Greetings! Your friends and neighbors have selected you to serve in the United States Army. Please report ..."

It was a career diversion dictated by the Korean War. Every draftee in America remembers that first day in the army. The farewell, tear smudged kisses from the girlfriend left behind, the long bus ride from Massachusetts to Fort Dix, New Jersey. The close-quarter line of buck naked men for the induction physical. The drafty World War II barracks. That shimmering Hollywood image of a somber faced, uniformed officer ringing my mother's doorbell, holding a telegram in one white-gloved hand and a neatly triangle folded flag in the other. That self-induced war-time paranoia that convinced me this was the first segment of the last segment of my young life.

In spite of these dramatic hallucinations, I managed to survive 16 weeks of basic training and the pressure of a commanding officer who tried to convince me to volunteer for Officers' Candidate School. He had appointed me a squad leader in my heavy weapons training company. But I had been following with more than casual interest the periodic publication of the names of war casualties. Many of them carried the prefix, Second Lieutenant, the newly minted products of Officers' Candidate school.

"Thank you, Sir. But I want to serve my two years and get back to a newspaper."

I had written to *Stars and Stripes* in Europe, the military newspaper, in the hope they would request me for a reporting assignment. I received a semi-encouraging response. If I were assigned anywhere in Europe, they would ask for my transfer to the staff. If not, sorry. In the time-honored G.I. confirmation of military logic, my orders were precisely in the opposite direction. I was bound for a heavy weapons infantry company in Korea. Because of a troop ship traffic jam at the embarkation port in Seattle, that westward journey was interrupted at Fort Sheridan, a military base outside of Chicago. We were in a holding pattern waiting for troopships to become available in the Pacific port.

Once more, the accident of timing. Chicago was the headquarters of the Fifth Army, one of four armies stationed in the United States. I knew they had a large public relations section that was responsible for all military publicity in the Midwestern states. But how to get to Chicago?

The top of the Fort Sheridan food chain may have been a distant base commander, but for me, confined to the barracks for transient personnel, the lynchpin of authority was an in-your-face Master Sergeant. He controlled every movement of his barracks kingdom, from the cockroaches to the most recent basic training graduates. Everything! From wake up reveille to the bugled taps at night. He was a huge, muscled black man who wore his yellow Master Sergeant stripes with a starched elegance that reflected that he was in an American army that had been desegregated by President Harry Truman less than 10 years earlier.

"Sarge," I said, after several anxious practice runs in front of the barrack's mirror. "I don't have a sick mother near here, I don't have a dying grandmother—matter of fact, I don't have a single relative within a thousand miles from this base. But I sure would appreciate a pass so I can see if I can get a job at Fifth Army Headquarters and get off this damn Heavy Weapons detail."

Of the conversational pauses I have known, this one ranks among the most enduring. "Soldier," the sergeant boomed, "You is the first mothah-fuckah who come here and tell me the truth. Be here at six hundred hours and pick up yo' pass."

Fifth Army Headquarters on Chicago's South Side was a startling revelation for a young soldier who just weeks earlier had been indoctrinated repeatedly with the military catechism, "salute everything that moves, pick up what doesn't, paint the rest."

The headquarters was a beehive of officers. They outnumbered the enlisted men. Captains, majors, a smattering of colonels; lieutenants swarmed in flocks of four and five. The only time I had ever seen a live major in the previous five months was on the Fort Dix parade ground, barking orders to a pre-dawn mass formation. My first up-close encounter with that brass was Major Pronjinski, the head of Fifth Army Public Affairs section.

"May, have you ever written any speeches?" He was perusing my double-spaced biographical offering, swathed in generous white space in an attempt to divert the eye from focusing on the slim collection of professional bench marks.

"We're looking for a speech writer... for the General."

"Well... " The pause was awkward while I weighed the moral collision between literary embellishment and a stark mental photograph of a heavy weapons platoon hunkered down on a Korean ridgeline.

"A few, Sir," I replied, hoping he would not press me for further details.

"I'm sure, Sir, I could get the hang of it in a short time." War and its consequences fortify the imagination, stretching it to its most creative limits.

"Let me find out if we can see the General," he dialed the phone.

There was a special elevator that took us to the Persian carpeted reception area of the General's suite. I remember the incongruity of Persian carpets in a military headquarters. Most of all, though, were those stars.

I had never seen anyone with three stars on each shoulder. Three stars in a single row! The symbols of rank reflected the room's sunlight. The General dismissed the major and, pointing to a couch, said, "May, sit down."

I'm not sure if I was dazzled more by those stars or the sudden realization that Private May, heavy weapons infantryman, was actually sitting down opposite a three-star general. Actually *sitting down*. Not standing at ramrod attention among hundreds of fellow soldiers!

Lt. Gen. Hobart R. Gay was not just one more general officer. He had been chief of staff to General George S. Patton, the World War II tank commander whose mechanized army swept into Germany. My about-to-be employer was with Patton when he was fatally injured in a Jeep accident while on a post-war hunting outing. The General, in months to come, would regale me with Patton stories as we outlined the skeletal form of his speeches. I would write them in the required military jargon of praise, patriotism and mediocrity, the latter ordained by an unbending rule of the chain of command. Not even a George S. Patton compatriot could deviate from what had never been uttered first by the Army Secretary or its Chief of Staff. Somehow, I rose to this cliché-forested occasion.

Military speechwriter.

More important, from my perspective, I was in America's Second City and not in some freezing bunker staring at the North Korean front lines. The riches of the city were in front of me, including the chance to resume my college education with a financial boost from the army. I enrolled in Northwestern University's Chicago campus night school, hitchhiking to class three times a week on Chicago's Outer Drive.

My professor, Ben Kartman, urged me to enter one of my magazine articles in a city-wide writing contest and subsequently celebrated my winning as enthusiastically as I did. The award dinner was at an upscale, "good breeding," deep leather-chaired private club on Lake Shore Drive. I particularly recall the dramatic part of the event. They wouldn't let me in.

Because I was part of the public relations department, I thought I needed to wear my uniform to represent my country and its military defenders. The doorman didn't share that view. He didn't have a U.S. Army enlisted man on his guest list. Ben Kartman had to come out and verify that the soldier actually was the guest of honor.

My army pals celebrated the next night less, I always thought, because of the writing award, and more because an army private—the guy sleeping in an upper bunk down the row—had stormed this inner sanctum of privilege and rank.

At the end of my military career and nighttime academic pursuits, I had made sufficient headway so I had only a year and a half of college remaining for my degree. It was a mere nine year span since that first obituary writing disaster at Columbia University's night school. The day after I was mustered out of the army I enrolled, for the first time, at a real—daytime—sprawling, trimmed-lawn university campus.

I was on the Northwestern University main Evanston campus, at the Medill School of Journalism. It was possible because of that crucial government thank-you-for-your-military-service, the G.I. Bill of Rights. All tuition was paid, plus a regular, every four-week support check of $122.

Less than two years later I was back to writing creative resumes from what now was my New York base. This time, however, I was armed with not only an additional line as a commanding general's speechwriter, but also with a crisp, framed parchment that said I was a college graduate.

In a burst of enthusiasm, I bought a sheet of 100 stamps to broadcast my talents to scores of journalism emporiums. This time, not just confined to New England. A smattering of responses arrived, including one from my most coveted choice, the *Washington Post*. It was a form letter. "Dear Sir," it said. My name already had slipped into the trashcan of anonymity. "We regret that we have no current openings…"

Maybe it was that immigrant gene that strains at every barrier, or just plain stubbornness packaged in optimism, but I bought a $13 ticket on the Eastern Airlines New York–Washington shuttle. I called from the airport. By some magical alignment of the stars, the *Washington Post* telephone operator put me through to the editor's office. There was enough magic left over to dust his executive secretary who forwarded the call.

"Yes?" the voice said.

"I'm calling from National Airport. I got your letter that there were no jobs in your newsroom, but I wanted to come down to have you get a look at me, just in case something might come up. Could you give me a few minutes?"

"You mean you flew to Washington even after we told you that we had no openings?" The rejoinder was wrapped in the tone of an incredulous question.

"Yes."

Again, there was that empty silence. "Come in," the editor said.

Apparently there is a common rhythm to job interviews. It is a format not unlike the first view of Niagara Falls. You're either in a tourist boat enjoying the spectacle, or you're in a bobbing barrel as a participant. These conversations start on a note of courtesy. Shortly after the opening banter, you either catch a rising air current of cautious hope or are buffeted by a down draft of rapidly developing gloom. Mine found some rising air even though the interview began with a clear reminder of the form letter: no openings. Fifteen minutes later we were still talking and I thought I was in a substantial updraft.

"I want you to talk to our managing editor and to take a small test we give to all editorial applicants," the editor said.

"Test? What test?" I asked, suddenly seeing myself clothed only in a barrel bobbing on the raging, foam crested current. I explained as diplomatically as I could that I didn't do well on tests like that. That I found myself weighing each multiple choice and all possible answers while the clock keeps ticking, eventually running out of minutes. I reached back to explain that Northwestern University had an admissions test just like his. I had scored so poorly that they let me in on probation even though the resume in front of him showed that later I graduated first in my class.

"Don't worry. You'll do fine. Take the test, get some lunch and come back and see me."

The moment I was back in his office, his reconfigured expression told of the downdraft gloom before he could even give the final benediction. You were right, he said. You didn't do well on the test. Sorry. He explained that since they began testing, all those who did well on the test did well in the news room.

What the hell, I thought, scanning the splintered barrel staves on the bottom of my Niagara Falls imagination. I asked a clearly interview-ending question, "How many reporters have you hired who flunked your test to see how they would do in your news room?"

I don't recall if he shook my hand or just opened the door to facilitate my exit. A few years later, a newspaper friend of mine sent that editor a *New York Times* clipping announcing that year's Pulitzer Prize winners. He stapled a note next to my picture, "Remember this guy? He flunked your journalism aptitude test."

Happily, the *Buffalo Evening News* had not yet warmed to aptitude testing. I found a home there that would change my life. With the largest editorial staff in the state outside of New York City, it prided itself as a newspaper of record, complete, detailed sometimes eye-glazing record. It vacuumed every dust ball of information, extracting from it at least a semblance of a news item. If you were elected acting treasurer of your neighborhood school's PTA, you read about it in the *News* the next day. A court appearance on a minor traffic infraction found your name in cold type. A police record about your missing cat? The next day your name and the cat's would be recorded for the edification of the western New York subscribers.

The *Buffalo Evening News* didn't stint on covering the big stories either. Its bulging advertising columns gave it the resources to do a professional job. I was sent to Canada to cover Queen Elizabeth's royal fanfare tour of neighboring Ontario province. And during the 1960 Presidential election, I was assigned to cover John F. Kennedy as he barnstormed through New York State, leaving a swath of squealing, adrenalin pumped female voters in his wake. I still have the dented portable typewriter, its scar sustained when one of them leaped over the barrier into the press box in Syracuse.

At the *Buffalo Evening News* there was only one journalistic religion: accuracy—worshiped, venerated, absolute accuracy. Generations of reporters learned about the significance of a middle initial as an indispensable part of the human anatomy, without which the person, more importantly, the story about him, was blatantly incomplete. The same dark shadow would blacken a reporter who called a piece of geography a "street" when it actually was christened an "avenue" in the well-worn City Directory. My enduring respect for middle initials, and the distinction between avenues, streets, roads, lanes, drives is a lifetime legacy of the *Buffalo Evening News.*

Like all newspapers, the *News* had its own idiosyncrasies. Fortunately, I received some warning about one of them before I started my journey through the job interviews. These began with the managing editor, shifted to the city editor, and, culminated at the desk of the executive editor, Alfred H.

Kirchhofer, whose mere name with its required German pronunciation, signaled authority. It was Paul Neville, the managing editor who alerted me.

"The chair," he said. "The chair you'll sit in at Mr. Kirchhofer's desk. Don't try to move it. It's bolted to the floor."

Later I learned the editor had an overwhelming concern about health. His own. Particularly and especially, germs—infectious germs he might catch. He ordered the chair, installed at a safe distance, securely bolted to the floor so there was no chance for any chair creep.

Alfred H. Kirchhofer and Paul Neville were professional newspapermen. They were proud of their work and their newspaper. Even though the *Buffalo Evening News* had some substantial competition from another daily, the *Buffalo Courier Express*, it was the lead voice of western New York. Statewide politicians regularly would come by to pay homage, a ritual that didn't necessarily lead to more generous coverage. The editors gave reporters leeway to develop complex stories and financed their travel throughout the state if they thought the issue was important enough.

After I wrote a series about the shortcomings of New York state adoption laws, a series picked up by other papers, it initiated an investigation by a committee of the New York State Senate. The editors sent me to four New York cities to cover the senate committee's public hearings. It was these articles that prompted a phone call from a Welfare Department caseworker and a discreet meeting in a nondescript coffee shop. Confidentiality and anonymity were a pre-condition.

"You ought to look at our department. It's a mess. We can't do our job. I'm not helping these families. I'm just handing out money. I've got too many cases, and keep getting more because of so much staff turnover," the source said. "You ought to get a job here and find out for yourself!"

It was a proposal that stuck with me. I discussed it with the managing editor. This was no small decision for a newspaper. Smuggle a reporter into the Welfare Department? Don't acknowledge his real identity? Devote three to six months of investigative reporting for just one series of articles? It was a decision of magnitude that required the approval of both the editor and the *Buffalo News'* owner. A week later I had an answer: apply for the job.

In two weeks I was a caseworker in the Erie County Department of Welfare with an overwhelming caseload. Even if I'd had the skills, I couldn't have handled it. Because I had previously written stories about the department and interviewed several of its employees, including its director, I had applied under a new name and altered my appearance.

The new caseworker was E. Preston May, who answered to the name of "Pret." The abbreviated version was calculated. Calling myself Henry or George was so foreign to my given name of Ed, I probably wouldn't turn around if I were called.

The physical transformation was another matter. I got a crew cut, had an optometrist make up a pair of black-framed glasses with plain window glass, and grew a mustache, dual disguises that harbored their own problems. In the first week, wearing the glasses gave me a terrific headache because my eyes would not look through the window glass, but focused, instead, on the large black frames.

Then there was the mustache. It grew out blond—so light colored that an observer had to be in total stare down mode to even notice it. A black eyebrow pencil fixed it. Every morning before leaving for my new social work job, I touched up that faintly visible bush under my nose to restore it to its intended bristling blackness. It worked. Even my mother had to take a second look when she first was startled by my new persona.

But the life of an imposter is not just a simple character change. I learned quickly that it is a challenge to eliminate a living person without the aid of cyanide or a pistol. My old self kept popping up. The first incident arrived during the first week of my newly fabricated self. My colleagues on the *News* staff were told I had quit suddenly. An emergency. A serious family illness. Poof! I vanished. From one day to the next. My newsroom friends, nurtured on the mother's milk of journalistic suspicion, didn't believe it. They wanted our union's executive committee, of which I had been a member, to launch an investigation. Luckily, the managing editor was able to slow that down with the venerable tactic of delay.

Weeks later, in what I was sure was a validation of Robert Burn's observation that "there is not such uncertainty as a sure thing," my tucked away past exploded into the present. I received a letter telling me that the person in temporary storage was to report for jury duty, without fail at 8 a.m. the following week. I ignored the summons. To this day, I never heard from them again.

But these inexplicably timed events tend not to travel in lonely splendor. A few weeks later I had a minor fender bender in which the other party insisted we file a police report. The next morning the *Buffalo Evening News*, ever the historian of record, reported, "Edgar May of 45 Mulberry St, yesterday was involved..." Fortunately, that day, my former staff colleagues were among the readers who did not peruse the paper with the fidelity its editors hoped for.

Meanwhile, I reported daily to my desk at the Welfare Department. Every evening I would transcribe my notes of the day's events. Three months later, in one of my occasional clandestine meetings with the managing editor, I told him that I had more than enough to document the series.

The letter of resignation to my Welfare Department supervisor told again of a family crisis that required me to return to Massachusetts. Once again, the unexpected: my coworkers organized a surprise farewell party, complete with a huge cake festooned with a marzipan "Good Luck!" on its pastry cream surface.

The farewell party added to what already was a growing moral quandary: had I morphed into a bona fide investigative reporter or simply into a latter day Benedict Arnold? It made the mandatory, inevitable phone call even more difficult. Late one afternoon after several months of writing and editing the 14 part series, I dialed the number of my former supervisor. The first installment would appear the next day in bold, black page one headlines.

"Yes, yes. I'm fine," I told my former supervisor. "I'm calling because I wanted you to know that tomorrow's *News* will carry a story... " There were no linguistic euphemisms, no cushion to soften this conversation. None. I provided the details. We said goodbye.

Some months later I was somewhat comforted by the results of the series. The County government raised staff salaries, added caseworkers that reduced caseloads, increased worker training, and expanded job entry requirements. The impetus for reforms received some unexpected national exposure. The Associated Press, the premier national wire service, distributed a shorter version of the series that was published by a significant number of newspapers around the country. Editorial writers weighed in with sharp elbow prose.

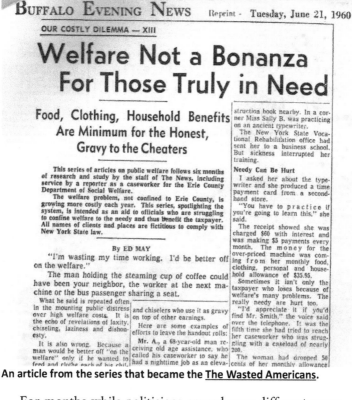

BUFFALO EVENING NEWS   Reprint - Tuesday, June 21, 1960

OUR COSTLY DILEMMA — XIII

Welfare Not a Bonanza For Those Truly in Need

Food, Clothing, Household Benefits Are Minimum for the Honest, Gravy to the Cheaters

This series of articles on public welfare follows six months of research and study by the staff of The News, including service by a reporter as a caseworker for the Erie County Department of Social Welfare.

The welfare problem, not confined to Erie County, is growing more costly each year. This series, spotlighting the system, is intended as an aid to officials who are struggling to confine welfare to the needy and thus benefit the taxpayer. All names of clients and places are fictitious to comply with New York State law.

By ED MAY

"I'm wasting my time working. I'd be better off on the welfare."

The man holding the steaming cup of coffee could have been your neighbor, the worker at the next machine or the bus passenger sharing a seat.

What he said is repeated often, in the mounting public distress over high welfare costs. It is the echo of revelations of laxity, chiseling, laziness and dishonesty.

It is also wrong. Because a man would be better off "on the welfare" only if he wanted to feed and clothe each of his chil- and chiselers who use it as gravy on top of other earnings.

Here are some examples of efforts to leave the handout rolls:

Mr. A., a 68-year-old man receiving old age assistance, who called his caseworker to say he had a nighttime job as an eleva-

struction book nearby. In a corner Miss Sally B. was practicing on an ancient typewriter.

The New York State Vocational Rehabilitation office had sent her to a business school. But sickness interrupted her training.

Needy Can Be Hurt

I asked her about the typewriter and she produced a time payment card from a second-hand store.

"You have to practice if you're going to learn this," she said.

The receipt showed she was charged $60 with interest and was making $5 payments every month. The money for the over-priced machine was coming from her monthly food, clothing, personal and household allowance of $35.95.

Sometimes it isn't only the taxpayer who loses because of welfare's many problems. The really needy are hurt too.

"I'd appreciate it if you'd find Mr. Smith," the voice said over the telephone. It was the fifth time she had tried to reach her caseworker who was struggling with a caseload of nearly 200.

The woman had dropped 50 cents of her monthly allowance

An article from the series that became the <u>The Wasted Americans</u>.

For months while politicians argued over different remedies, I was told to continue covering the story until I was sure there were only three readers left—the copy editor, the managing editor and my mother. Even I was beginning to get weary until...

It was the following May. I had an inkling that the editors had submitted the series for the pinnacle of journalism honors, the Pulitzer Prize. I was long schooled in the verity of "many are called, few are chosen." There were many nominees in each category. I also knew about the ritual. The awards would be announced at three o'clock of the designated afternoon. I tried to hang around the paper's glass enclosed wire room, as nonchalantly as possible, fooling nobody.

A minute or so after 3 pm I heard the repeated ringing of the machine's bell, a warning that a major news bulletin was about to arrive.

"Pulitzer Prizes," the tap, tap of the machine announced. It printed each of the winners in their special categories. Tap... tap... tap...

E-d-g-a-r M-a-y... I really don't remember much about what happened next. The newsroom erupting in a shouting, backslapping melee. The sound of popping champagne corks. Again, the accident of coincidence challenging reality—the Columbia University official who was quoted in the bulletin announcing the awards was the secretary of the Pulitzer Prize Committee. His name was John Hohenberg, my night school professor who had looked askance at my very first journalistic outing—that obituary. Some years later he told me he had momentarily thought of giving me an early alert about the award, but, on reflection, concluded that would be bending the rules. But there was no doubt about his paternal feelings; his former night school student was among the honorees.

The formal part of the newsroom celebration ended with a brief speech by chair-bolted-to-the-floor Editor-In-Chief Alfred H. Kirchhofer. I vaguely remember the hazy image of a smile, an emergence about as common as his overlooking an errant or missing middle initial.

Four weeks later, after the hullabaloo had calmed, we would have a conversation. He was wearing his green eye shade, adding emphasis to the gravity of the subject: we talked about money. My money. I noted my appreciation of the $500 bonus I received after the prizes were announced. But every week since then, I explained, I had looked hopefully at the details of my weekly paycheck… But… nothing, no change. There it was again. That awkwardly entombed silence that seems to have attached itself to my most difficult conversations.

"Hmm… Yes, we need to give you a raise. What do you have in mind?"

"After the Pulitzer," I said, with a white-knuckle grip on the bolted chair, "I thought I might be able to earn $10,000 a year in the newspaper business." Another soundless void, but this time longer and more somber than the first.

His lips were pursed. An index finger tapped the eye shade. "Well… in that case, you might want to consider working at our television station."

You tend to remember a conversation that shifts the trajectory of your life. This was one of them. It nagged at me, persistently, like an itch you just can't quite reach. For me to earn $10,000 a year I had to leave the newspaper business and become a performer, a television personality, complete with a daily, pre-airtime appointment with the makeup lady. That image combined with a stored picture of a seminal event more than a year earlier.

It happened after my series on New York State adoption problems had prompted a state senate investigation. It was *our* story, and the *Buffalo News* had sent me to cover the committee hearings. One of them was in the courthouse in Brooklyn.

I was as puffed up as only a barely-out-of-his-twenties reporter can be, finding himself seated in the press box with "the big boys." An elderly man took the seat next to me. (At barely 30, everybody older looked a bit wrinkled and "elderly.") With all the studied casualness I thought was called for, I extended my hand.

"Edgar May, *Buffalo News*," I said.

"Homer Bigart, the *Times*," he answered.

Homer Bigart!

The Homer Bigart? Sitting right there next to me, reporting the same story as I was, reporting it for the *New York Times!* Homer Bigart was one of my journalism heroes. He had been the *Time's* war correspondent in Korea, a prize winning star who was on the front page almost every day. I was actually sitting next to Homer Bigart!

Later that night I had sifted through the day's events, including my proximity to my hero. The adoption story was important to me, pulse-raising important. Having written a series that led to a state investigation was, for a relative newcomer to journalism, ego boosting. But, for Homer Bigart—famous war correspondent? It was, at best, a second rate news item for the *Times*. An assistant city editor had scanned the vast *Times* news room for a body to cover a marginal story. Homer Bigart was sitting at his desk, reading the paper. He became the random choice.

The memory blended awkwardly with the conversation with my chair-bolted-to-the-floor editor. As we talked about television news, I recalled the image of the elderly man sitting

Working on The Wasted Americans.

next to me in a Brooklyn Court House, in the waning years of his exemplary reporting career. *That! That's not going to happen to me.* These paired truths collided with the conviction that my newspaper years never seemed like work. Almost every assignment was an adventure, with the possible exception of a couple of obituaries. Every day was a chance to be an eyewitness of the frailties of humankind and, in contrast, the strength of the human condition. I never regretted this whirligig adventure, but following in the aging path of Homer Bigart? Like a fading love affair whose heart skipping moments are still too vivid to obscure the hurt, I knew this segment of my life's story had ended.

With niece Julia Kunin in 1962, around the time his book was published.

CHAPTER FIVE

Sarge

My secretary already had her coat on for her weekend departure when she rushed through the door with what I thought was more than an end of week animated expression on her face.

"You have a call from Washington. It's Sargent Shriver, the head of the Peace Corps!"

"I read your book last night," the voice said, "and I want to know how long are you going to criticize this problem and when are you going to do something about it?"

Just like that. No euphemisms. No diplomatic schmaltz to help slide into the core subject.

"What is it you would like me to do about it?"

"I'd like you to come down here so we can talk," said President John F. Kennedy's brother-in-law. "What are you doing tomorrow? No. Wait. I just looked at my Saturday schedule—can't do it tomorrow. Sunday? What are you doing Sunday?"

My book, The Wasted Americans, had shown up on Shriver's bedside table in his night reading collection. It had just been published and had received an encouraging number of reviews. It was built on the foundation of the *Buffalo Evening News* series. The book, however, expanded a regional story into a national recitation of discomfort. The message? Poverty in our country was real, often camouflaged in the dusty, sometimes hidden cracks of want, rarely visible within the vaunted landscape of prosperity in America. It joined Michael Harrington's The Other America, a powerful portrayal of neglect that told Americans what they didn't want to hear.

In that moment of Shriver's call I was unaware that I just had been introduced to the seamless, undetectable boundary that was meant to separate days of the week, but was an invisible border between weekends and work days, a proprietary distinction of any Kennedy Family calendar. The Shriver time piece that could never distinguish between work and rest was personally reinforced for me about a year later when he reluctantly, very reluctantly, acquiesced to a personal request. We had concluded our usual morning discussion of the latest poverty firestorms, when I told him I wanted to bring up a special matter.

"Yes?" he said.

"I'm going to get married."

"You're going to do *what*?"

The question mark at the end of the sentence clearly signaled that my announcement was a breach of Poverty War patriotism because it required a week's absence from the front lines. After a congratulatory handshake he reluctantly let me take the time off for my honeymoon in Switzerland. Midway, he wanted to get some information from me but couldn't find me. Sarge summoned Interpol, the international police agency, for a search. It failed. I had rented a car in Zurich under my wife's maiden name.

Sarge Shriver had just been appointed by President Lyndon B. Johnson to a second job as head of the President's task force on the War on Poverty. As a member of that small, exclusive Presidential team, he had access to those special power baubles that are the unique ego flattering properties of the White House. They were apparent that early Sunday morning in 1964 when I arrived at Washington's National Airport. The man in the black chauffeur's uniform held a sign that said "May." The small, metal tag on his cap told of his employer, "The White House."

There are more conventional first meetings than ours. My arrival at Shriver's Maryland home was announced not only by the black White House car in the semi-circle driveway, but by the ringing of the doorbell... ringing, ringing, ringing... the button was stuck. My first impression of the director of the Peace Corps was a man wielding a huge butcher knife. Our first joint venture was prying the button loose from its jammed surroundings.

The interview flowed precisely in the channels Shriver had in mind. He was a powerful persuader. In the pre-inauguration days of the Kennedy White House years, he had been one of his brother-in-law's most effective talent scouts. He persuaded Robert S. McNamara to become Secretary of Defense, seven months after McNamara had been named head of one of the country's top corporations, the Ford Motor Company.

With me, the job was a lot easier. Within an hour after the White House "treatment" and the doorbell serenade, I agreed to come to Washington as a special assistant to the director of the President's task force on the War on Poverty. I would come for thirty days. It appeared to have been an underestimate. Our association lasted about ten years.

Sargent Shriver and Edgar with unidentified man around 1965.

President Johnson didn't pick Shriver to head the War on Poverty just because of his record with the popular Peace Corps or his family connection to the Kennedys. President Johnson understood the mood of Congress—the foibles and strengths of each of its diverse members—better than any other recent president. He chose Sarge because he had the credibility and political skills to gather a majority of "Yes" votes for what Johnson knew would be a controversial law.

In the gestation stage of the Peace Corps, Shriver had mounted a dazzling spectacle of political persuasion. In a blitz that may have been a first in executive branch lobbying, he met personally with every single member of Congress, all 435 House members and each of the 100 senators. The effort became a regular part of our morning coffee conversation.

As an encore he buffed his own, and the Peace Corps', reputation among the Congress with a gesture that occurred in Washington about as frequently as the sighting of Halley's Comet: at the end of the year he actually returned unspent Peace Corps dollars to the United States Treasury.

This was not simply a display of unaccustomed frugality. It fashioned a political strategy that helped nudge unconvinced legislators toward a "Yes" vote for the new anti-poverty law. It included Shriver's knack, no, zest, for exploiting going on the cheap. He insisted that any dollar spent by the Presidential task force be clearly an act of last resort. If you want to create a new government program to do something about poverty in America, you can't cherish—and certainly can't flaunt—the usual bric-a-brac of Washington décor that trumpets rank and status: No window-draped offices, no lush carpets, no cocktail tables displaying large art books that were never read. And, during the task force days, no paychecks for the new private sector recruits.

As task force "volunteers" we were hidden in a variety of Washington cubbyholes, like moles burrowing in windowless cellars, in offices temporarily converted from their preordained life of storage. To implement this frugality, Shriver enlisted a couple of enforcers who knew Washington's hidden bureaucratic sleights of hand as well as they knew their own children. Bill Kelly, a veteran skillful government operator, was our management chieftain. His consigliore was Emidio Tini, a master scrounge. Tini grew up in South Philadelphia where kindergarten was preceded by a mandatory neighborhood street course in Darwinian survival of not just the fittest, but the most agile.

Kelly and Tini located "donated" space, and the basic furniture for these offices. Dozens of desks, chairs, and an assortment of sometimes slightly blemished conference tables all poured out of government trucks that Tini had requisitioned from his pals in other agencies.

On the day Shriver was sworn in as the director of the new Office of Economic Opportunity, we suddenly realized we didn't have the necessary Bible. Within 30 minutes Emidio Tini produced one—brand new, pristine, still sealed inside its tight cellophane wrapping. He'd purloined it from a Department of Commerce warehouse which didn't seem to have a use for it.

But in the frenetic pre-congressional action days of the President's task force on the War on Poverty, the lack of the Good Book, was not a priority. The possible lack of a House of Representatives majority vote was the only issue. From whatever nook or cranny we were hidden, we were hustling for "Yes" votes. Our lobbying team filtered every single legislative player, no matter how obscure, through the "Yes or No" voter screen. We were energized by Shriver's vaunted salesmanship, and also aided by the fact that Sarge's young, talented deputy, Bill Moyers, recently had been commandeered to the White House as a key aide to President Johnson.

The President himself—whose arm twisting with members of Congress was legendary—joined the effort. Even the certain "No" votes received his attention. He ordered that recently constructed federal buildings, like court houses and post offices in a recalcitrant congressman's district, would be formally dedicated on the day of the poverty vote. Obviously, the dedication ceremony required the presence of the congressman who made the building possible. Ever solicitous, the President offered government aircraft to ferry the legislators to their districts. I always suspected the pilots were instructed not to return to Washington until after the final poverty program vote was tallied. An absent vote was a lot better than a recorded "No" vote.

Lyndon Johnson may have inherited the planning of the new anti-poverty effort from John F. Kennedy on that national day of grieving the previous November, but he made it his own priority. He didn't need Michael Harrington's or my book to document America's unfinished work of converting the country's patriotic slogans of equality to the reality of daily life—daily life for *all* Americans.

Johnson understood the gap between rhetoric and reality. He learned it, first hand, growing up without electricity or indoor plumbing. He saw the inequities every morning as a young teacher in his Cotulla, Texas classroom where Mexican–American children arrived in the morning with the patches of poverty on their sometimes threadbare go-to-school clothes. [1]

"Somehow you never forget what poverty and hatred can do when you see its scars on the hopeful face of a child," he told America and a joint session of Congress:

> "I never thought then, in 1928, that I would be standing here in 1965. It never even occurred to me in my fondest dreams, that I might have the chance to help the sons and daughters of those students and to help people like them all over the country. But now I do have that chance—and I'll let you in on a secret—I mean to use it." [2]

Lyndon Baines Johnson was a towering complex of contradictions that were far taller than his 6 foot 4 inch frame. He hovered over those he intended to persuade or, alternatively, to intimidate, like an over-sized curving exclamation point that precariously leaned into his quarry.

Among all the books and articles that are an expanding library of analysis and psychological parsing about this President, maybe a one sentence summary comes closest to defining this complex giant. Comparing him to his debonair and articulate slain predecessor, Liz Carpenter, a fellow Texan, family friend and close confidant, offers an incisive summary:

> I have always thought that you could describe presidents in almost a word. Kennedy inspired, which Johnson was not capable of doing, and Johnson delivered. [3]

On January 8, 1964 he turned a hidden, often ignored national embarrassment into an American priority:

> This administration today, here and now, declared unconditional war on poverty in America. I urge this Congress and all Americans to join me in that effort.

> It will not be a short or easy struggle, no single weapon or strategy will suffice, but we shall not rest until that war is won. The richest nation on earth can afford to win it. We cannot afford to lose it. [4]

The Economic Opportunity Act passed 247–182 August 20, 1964.

The bill signing ceremony was in the sun-illuminated Rose Garden in front of the Oval Office. Sarge had put my name on the list of the small group that would accompany him. After signing multiple copies, the President shook my hand. He thanked me for helping the legislation become law. And then he handed me one of the pens he had used to affirm it.

It is an enduring picture... the antique desk where the President signed the bill... the flowers, like a Renaissance painting, a profusion of blooming roses... the precisely manicured green lawns. But not the speeches, I don't remember the speeches. They're a blur. I was transfixed by my surroundings, emotionally smothered by them. I actually, yes, actually was in the President's house!

I remember standing there amid the Senate and House leaders who I recognized from their pictures in the newspapers, surrounded by a profusion of television cameras, the flashes of intense light from the squadron of news photographers.

Days later, after the euphoria of victory faded, some of us were convinced that the vote count was more because of Sarge's and the Peace Corps' reputation than the content of this euphemistically christened law. This assessment gained currency in the first couple of budget cycles. Members of Congress began to understand that the innocently labeled Economic Opportunity Act actually meant that black and white children would go to school together, even in the South; rowdy urban youth would be in special training camps, occasionally ogling the local girls in neighboring rural small towns.

Most unsettling to both urban and rural politicians alike was that seemingly innocent legislative phrase which mandated decision making "with maximum feasible participation of the poor." It meant you had to put poor, neighborhood folks on boards that decided what programs were good for them and where limited poverty dollars would go. By the time the congressional phone calls to Shriver and the White House had turned into a chorus of concern, Sarge had appointed me Inspector General of the War on Poverty, the ultimate depository of these distress calls.

In his Peace Corps days, Sarge Shriver had a large sign on his office door: "Bring me only bad news. Good news weakens me." We never felt the need to take that sign with us when we moved permanently to the War on Poverty offices. Certainly my office rarely disappointed him about fulfilling those instructions; every day the verity of "unintended consequences" black-clouded my desk.

In West Virginia, the first contingent of VISTA volunteers, the Peace Corps' domestic counterpart, were determined to change life for the better in the coal-grimy hollows separating the scarred, strip-mined hills. It didn't take them long to learn that the elected local judge was the feudal monarch in the county where he presided. The judge decided which road got paved and, more significantly, which applicant got the county job. Just as rapidly the volunteers calibrated which judge was on their side and which one was not. The newly minted volunteers also focused on remedies—encourage those who are helpful and discourage those who are not. They began to register voters. Lots of new voters.

Now, the first requirement of an effective political leader—whether in urban Chicago or in rural West Virginia—is to know your voters. More to the point, know they will vote for you or your candidate. A large crowd of new voters is a nerve-jangling enigma in that political equation. The new unknowns are liable to vote for any—*any*—candidate on the ballot!

The next congressional reauthorization of the anti-poverty law included a West Virginia political peace offering: our volunteers were prevented, by legislative edict, from registering voters.

There were other impediments.

In Mississippi the Office of Inspection recorded some vivid brush strokes on the national portrait of a wrenching civil rights struggle. The U.S. Department of Agriculture was providing states with surplus food from its storage warehouses. The food was free but the individual states had to pay for distributing it. The governor of Mississippi, aware that the majority of the surplus food recipients were poor blacks, ended the program because he said the state didn't have the money to pay for distributing the food. After a call from civil rights leaders, Shriver phoned the governor and told him the anti-poverty program would pay for food distribution.

There remained one substantial problem: The new Civil Rights law said no federal dollars can go to a segregated program. The Mississippi Welfare Department had exactly one black employee, a janitor at its Jackson headquarters. There were none in its 124 county welfare departments. Shriver told me to make sure the local departments had black employees so we would meet the requirement of the new Civil Rights Act. The instructions had more clarity than the solution.

I saw my counterpart at the Department of Agriculture to discuss a loan of some of his inspectors. He had a bigger inspection staff in his Atlanta regional office alone than I had nationwide. The reception was lukewarm, cooled by the reality that the chairmen of congressional committees overseeing agriculture all had southern roots, nurtured in the soil of segregation.

Occasionally, just occasionally, there is some encouraging evidence that God sides with the good, even when the good use a bit of stealth and exaggeration. Those turned out to be the necessary tools. I assembled about a third of my lean staff, supplementing them with volunteer bodies from other parts of our agency. The instructions were simple: go to Jackson. Register in separate motels. Take your portion of the Mississippi Welfare Department office list. Call each county commissioner. Identify yourself as a Federal Inspector and request an appointment to discuss the food distribution effort. Be sure to ask for directions to the commissioner's office and the name of a good motel in his town.

It was clear that with 124 county offices, we could make only a fraction of those appointments. But the Mississippi welfare system was convinced that a swarm of federal locusts had descended on the state. They seemed to be scheduled everywhere. Within two weeks we received confirmation that black warehousemen and black loading dock helpers were on the payroll. We had integrated the department.

In the roll call of unexpected consequences, this incident was only one example where the War on Poverty became an unwitting catalyst of the Civil Rights movement. Passionate and, sometimes, vitriolic political debates about race may have been centered in Washington, but the flashpoints of their angry content exploded in neighborhoods that first hosted the new poverty programs. The fragile strands of equality where inequality had thrived were the tinder that ignited the bonfires of prejudice: blacks versus whites, Latinos versus Anglos, American Indians versus their neighboring ranchers.

Nearly half a century later, with a black president and his huge electoral majority behind him, these events of the Sixties seem like surreal, fictional snippets. They are not.

They were real, stark, repetitive, often bloody footprints on the stop-and-start road to equality. Most days they were recorded in my routine War on Poverty "incident" files.

> -A three a.m. wake up call from the FBI's Washington office night supervisor with a suggestion that I might want to get a couple of inspectors to a small town in Alabama. Twelve hours earlier there was a community meeting in a local black church to consider applying for a Head Start grant that would have to be bi-racial. By midnight the church had been burned to the ground.

> -In rural Kentucky, a new Job Corps center made the "incident" list because of "unforeseen circumstances" that training program planners never envisioned. Job Corps' black staff members could not find a place to live in the small rural towns surrounding the center. No landlord would rent to a black family. None. Suddenly, we were in the housing business. We brought in house trailers and built a staff compound inside the center's fenced perimeter.

Incidents like these sometimes were not clear cut or one-sided. Some were rooted in the fractious thickets of race relations that were increasingly heated by emotions boiling on both sides. The most publicized of these racial cauldrons was a state wide Head Start program, the largest of its kind, the Child Development Group of Mississippi [CDGM].

We became aware of the turmoil when Sarge Shriver was called to the ornate Senate office of Mississippi's John C. Stennis, a Washington power broker of the first rank, and chairman of the Armed Services Committee. Sarge asked me to accompany him because the summons clearly was an Inspection issue. The Senator, a white-maned patrician, had a mellifluous deep southern drawl that registered with an adopted Yankee like me. From his point of view, I was sure he thought I "spoke funny."

"Saahge, Edgah," he opened, "Ah know what you're tryin' to do, but your nevah, nevah goin' to have Nigra chillun going to school with white chillun in the state of Mississippi."

There was no rancor in his voice. No theatrics for emphasis. John Stennis was a reflection of his native southern culture, not an echo of the incessant drum beat of racism, propelled into the black headlines of intolerance. Unlike some of his political brethren, he did not thunder the contemporary litany, repeatedly, before any segregationist audience.

He turned the discussion over to his chief aide, a professional investigator who methodically outlined his evidence that CDGM was not just a large Head Start organization, but one that illegally used federal dollars to promote a Civil Rights agenda. He said that Head Start teachers' aides, paid to be in Mississippi classrooms, actually were in the North raising money for civil rights.

The Senator gave us a week to investigate the claims. They were true. Documented with payroll records and signed time sheets. There was no wiggle room. No possible explanation. I recommended that we had no choice but to stop funding Mississippi's statewide Head Start program and immediately create an alternative. If not, the national publicity about misused federal dollars could endanger all the poverty programs. Shriver agreed.

A few weeks later we began to understand this emotional uproar was expanding both within and outside of the Civil Rights community. We were meeting with CDGM's Head Start leadership in our Atlanta Regional office to look for salvage options. It was an unpublicized effort with Shriver himself at the head of the conference table. Shortly after it started, a staff member asked me to step outside for a moment. "It's really important," she said.

On the other side of the door was the Reverend Dr. Martin Luther King. We shook hands and he asked if he could participate in the meeting. I responded that I would like to inform Mr. Shriver that he was there because I was sure Sarge would want to interrupt the discussion so he could come out and greet him.

The Shriver–Dr. King connection already had become part of political folklore. It was a prominent chapter in the history of President John F. Kennedy's narrow election victory. In the campaign hierarchy, Shriver had been the conduit to the nation's black leadership. In the last month of the campaign, the Rev. Dr. Martin Luther King was arrested and jailed at a Civil Rights rally in Selma. More than the Reverend's staff feared for his life. Shriver urged his brother-in-law to call Mrs. King and express his concern. It was a controversial recommendation. In spite of strong opposition from some campaign strategists, Jack Kennedy made the call. It resonated in the nation's black communities. Somebody important was paying attention. Somebody cared. Maybe the next president. In the post-election tea leaf readings, several political analysts said that phone call may have made the difference between a narrow victory and defeat.

But that morning in that Atlanta conference room, the drama of their converging past was superimposed by the tensions of the present. In welcoming Dr. King, Shriver informed the nation's charismatic Civil Rights leader that we were in the middle of a negotiation between the government and one of its major contractors. However, he would be pleased to interrupt the meeting to have Rev. King share his views.

Again, that pulse-racing moment of silence. It hung there, teetering between confrontation and accommodation. It was broken by a nod from Dr. King. The Reverend, in that deep, resonant voice of authority, talked about the chasm separating opportunity of black and white children growing up in America. The Mississippi Head Start program, he said, was among the important signs of hope and change. It had become larger than Mississippi. It was important to all of his people no matter where they happened to live. There were no octave risings that embellish a Sunday sermon. No thrusting of arms reaching for the sky. It was a simple, brief message that everyone in the room understood. Sarge thanked Dr. King and accompanied him, arm in arm, out of the conference room.

Within weeks, however, it was clear the tensions were rising and not diminishing over a Head Start program that had been propelled onto a national stage already cluttered with Civil Rights discord. A full page advertisement in the *New York Times* confirmed it: "Say It Isn't So, Sarge" it demanded. There was no mention of teachers' aides, paid with federal poverty dollars, who were supposed to be in Mississippi classrooms on the days they actually were in Chicago soliciting funds for civil rights. It had become clear that neither these facts nor government documents stamped "Confidential" blunted a decibel-rising emotional public debate. Even some of our own staff were among the protestors.

Shriver insisted that there would not be a shutdown order with only a government-issue letter. The notice needed to be handed personally to officials in Jackson by those of us responsible and would be delivered without public fanfare or press release to the Mississippi Head Start officials so they could prepare their public response. Predictably, there was a leak.

"Feds to Shutter CDGM," the *Jackson Daily News* announced when we arrived early in the morning at Jackson's airport. Our team included the heads of our agency's Community Action Program—responsible for Head Start, the Office of Inspection, the chief auditor, and a general counsel lawyer. One of our team was a black man, Theodore Berry, director of Community Action who years later would be the first black mayor of Cincinnati. Because of the early flight, none of us had breakfast. We stopped at a small roadside restaurant. I asked the others to wait while I went inside, ostensibly to find out if they could handle eight of us. But I had other concerns.

"Do you serve Negroes?" I asked the one waitress. She stared at me.

"We have to," was her response.

We divided ourselves into two booths and ordered breakfast. Our table had finished our breakfast while those at the other booth that included Ted Berry were still waiting for their order. They would wait another 45 minutes before the first cup of coffee was poured.

After conferring with the group, I said I wanted to call Shriver before we continued into the city. I reported that we had been set up. I told him about the morning news headlines and the insult to Ted Berry. We wanted his approval to abort the mission and close the program a few days later with a personal phone call and a follow-up official notice.

"Come back," Shriver said.

Because clarity sometimes comes only with distance, we didn't recognize it then but we already were on the downward slope of the War on Poverty. We seemed to be running in place, pinched between hugely increasing demands and frozen annual appropriations.

There was a one-word explanation: Vietnam. The war's voracious demands produced domestic casualties, and we suddenly found ourselves among the wounded. The ever-building military conflict brought a new kind of poverty to antipoverty programs—the poverty of misplaced, expanding, unfulfilled hope.

The War on Poverty, it turned out, was not to be a real war. It was crippled by the turmoil in Southeast Asia which was eroding our endeavor, turning a passionate skirmish with committed soldiers into an effort without the crucial supply lines to support our lofty battle plans. The mounting controversies and the shrinking resources expanded the hostile rhetoric. The preachers of right-wing conservatism found their microphones, sometimes reaching back for biblical support: "Go to the ant, thou sluggard; consider her ways, and be wise."

But there were both moderate and liberal voices that joined the chorus of discontent. In his book, Indomitable Will: LBJ in the Presidency, Mark Updegrove identifies the growing chasm between Lyndon Johnson and the Reverend Martin Luther King, who pointed directly at the culprit in a 1967 speech on Vietnam: The Civil Rights leader referred to the poverty program as being "broken and eviscerated as if it were some idle political plaything of a society gone mad on war."[5]

Among the terminally wounded was Lyndon Baines Johnson. On the evening of March 31, 1968, from his desk in the Oval Office, with a globe of the world in the background, the President addressed the nation. The agony of the war hung like a persistent fog over him. He closed his speech with these words:

> With American sons in the field far away, with the American future under challenge right here at home, with our hopes and the world's hopes for peace in the balance every day, I do not believe that I should devote an hour or a day of my time to any personal partisan causes or to any duties other than the awesome duties of this office, the Presidency of our country. Accordingly, I shall not seek, and I will not accept, the nomination of my party as your President.[6]

There were additional troubling complexities that confronted Americans. As the national poverty debate expanded, an ever larger cohort of citizens began to understand that poverty was not a germ you caught by not washing your hands, or by your proximity to a sneezing neighbor. Sometimes it was promoted by the very white-shirt-and-tie institutions we depend on: bankers who red-lined entire slum neighborhoods so that loans were simply not available in America's ghettos; school boards who acquiesced to assigning some of the most marginal and inexperienced teachers to the most needy schools; city politicians who turned a blind eye to their Building Departments as they sent the fewest inspectors to the poverty-scarred neighborhoods where they were needed most.

The answer to these embarrassing political disparities was an Office of Economic Opportunity that launched a frontal assault at the source of the problems: spending federal government poverty dollars to attack closer-to-home government dollars. Worse yet, the other dollars were doled out by elected mayors and council members who watched in dismay as the poverty warriors skirmished with their school boards, their building inspectors and sometimes with their police—both verbally and physically—when their followers' frustrations boiled over.

Neither side fully understood that we were in an era of seismic shifts in our society. "We shall overcome" and "burn, baby, burn" were more than sloganeering. They were the street cries that had become the hymnals of social change. They and the new poverty programs sometimes merged, not in tactics, but in purpose. We had become not only a magnet for the dispossessed, but a night light for the angry and their radical offspring.

I remember the first time I saw the widely distributed photo of Bobby Seale, the Black Panther leader. He was sitting in an oriental fan chair, holding a rifle with bandoliers of ammunition crossing his chest. My focus was sharpened when I was told he was on the payroll of one of our poverty programs. Not for long. We quietly hustled him off the manifest.

There were others. My favorite was Jesse Gray, a New York City no-holds-barred combatant who had a superb flair for publicity. In today's modern parlance, Jesse would be called a community organizer. He learned his trade as a rent-strike leader, creatively protesting Harlem's housing conditions. To make his point, he journeyed to the sedate, mahogany furnished New York court rooms where he sued his adversaries. To underline his ardor, he brought live and dead rats with him.

In our first year, he found time to focus his talents on the embryonic poverty program. He did it with such single-minded ferocity that it prompted our regional director, a former New York City deputy police commissioner, to arrive at work with his old service revolver strapped to his hip. One morning Jesse arrived at the regional office with a retinue of acolytes and a basket camouflaged by a raincoat. Once inside the reception area his troops emptied the basket and liberated the chickens it contained. Jesse welcomed them with handfuls of cracked corn he broadcast on the polished reception room floor.

A few feet behind him were the major news television cameras that Jesse, naturally, had alerted to the impending drama. Amid the whir of cameras and the clucking and the pecking. Jesse shouted, "Chicken feed! Chicken feed! That's what you're giving my people."

A short while later, flush with this publicity bonanza, Jesse took his high voltage, personal anti-poverty crusade national. He arrived at Washington's Capitol building with another team of followers, and another camouflaged basket. This time its contents suggested a replay of his rent-strike antics. Except the basket contained rats. Large, live rats. The plan was to toss them over the banister from the visitor's gallery on to the floor of the House of Representatives. The strategy was aborted when a House security officer asked to see what was in the basket.

For our Office of Inspection the story didn't end there. I was concerned about the particulars of the event. One of my New York inspectors identified them after sorting through stacks of invoices. They appeared in neatly typed letters:

Material for constructing rat cages $23.47

Food for rats $ 9.48

The rats were free. They came from Jesse's Harlem neighborhood.

Such vignettes of controversy became the journalistic fodder that fed the public image of the War on Poverty. Nearly a quarter of a century later, in another State of the Union speech, President Ronald Reagan, a master of the sound bite, said that his predecessor had declared war on poverty.

Poverty," he said, "won."

It was a widely quoted presidential quip. It also was widely off the mark. A year before the wounded Office of Economic Opportunity was interred—with most of its programs surviving and handed off to other federal agencies—poverty in America had reached its lowest level since the Census Bureau started keeping these statistics. It had dropped to 12.1% of the population, declining from 19% at the beginning of the Kennedy years.

In the intervening years as the gap widened between the affluent and the poor—particularly among America's children—those low numbers disappeared. In 2012 the U.S. Census Bureau reported that the number of poor in America had doubled since the end of the anti-poverty skirmish.

For me, however, this documented progress was about to become distant, suddenly no longer relevant. Because my Poverty War odyssey abruptly ended on a chilly November evening that was to become the most searing challenge of my life.

[1] Updegrove, M.K. 2012. *Indomitable Will: LBJ in the Presidency*. Crown, p. 144-145.

[2] Updegrove, 2012 (as n. 1 above), p. 145. [Lyndon B. Johnson speech cited: "Special Message to the Congress: The American Promise," March 15, 1965.]

[3] Updegrove, 2012 (as n. 1 above), p. 30.

[4] Lyndon B. Johnson: "Annual Message to the Congress on the State of the Union." January 8, 1964. Online by Gerhard Peters and John T. Woolley, *The American Presidency Project*. http://www.presidency.ucsb.edu/ws/?pid=26787.

[5] Updegrove, 2012 (as n. 1 above), p. 274. [Martin Luther King speech cited: "Beyond Vietnam: Time to Break Silence." Delivered April 4, 1967 at Riverside Church, New York City.]

[6] Lyndon B. Johnson: "The President's Address to the Nation Announcing Steps To Limit the War in Vietnam and Reporting His Decision Not To Seek Reelection," March 31, 1968. Online by Gerhard Peters and John T. Woolley, *The American Presidency Project*. http://www.presidency.ucsb.edu/ws/?pid=28772.

CHAPTER SIX

Accident

I don't remember the details. None of them. The violence. The crunching of metal, the shattered glass carpeting the macadam, the blinding, twitching blue lights. God—if you believe in God—has a special way of insulating tragedy. He doesn't remove the pain but somehow he collects the most jagged shards—one by one—sweeping them up and locking them away so you will never find them in the storage bin of your mind.

I don't remember who told me. Maybe I sensed it. About my wife. No one mentioned her name. Absolutely no one. When no one talks about what they know is most important to you, the silence holds its own unspoken conversation.

Later, much later, they told me about the ambulance rushing me to the local hospital. About my brother-in-law and friend, Arthur Kunin, who sped down from Burlington the 123 miles of darkened Interstate. The decision he and Sherburne Lovell, the orthopedic surgeon, made. If I were going to

live, it would take the greater expertise of Dartmouth-
Hitchcock Hospital, a key New England trauma center 35
minutes away. Arthur rode with me in the ambulance.

For three days I had been unconscious. Then a blurred
awakening: the rhythmic sound of the breathing machine that
was a stand-in for my punctured lung; the bright-lighted
numbers, multiple displays that were part of the forest of medical technology surrounding my bed; the white walls... and
uniformed nurses, wrapped in white and their professional
calm, the one assurance of humanity in this antiseptic portrait.

My first memory pictures after regaining consciousness
were of familiar faces: my mother, looking over my bed... the
faces of Sarge Shriver and Monsignor Geno Baroni, my friend
who had married Louise and me. I couldn't speak because of
the breathing tube in my throat. The flutter of my eyelids was
the only language I had to tell them that I knew they were in
the room. They, together with more than 40 co-workers, had
chartered an airplane to attend the funeral. Msgr. Baroni was a
co-celebrant of the Mass for Louise.

Geno Baroni was the highest ranking priest in the United
States government. It's a distinction that still is accurate. He
was an Assistant Secretary of Housing and Urban Affairs. Later he was a key political operative for Jimmy Carter in his
presidential election campaign. Not only was he a popular
priest in a large Catholic Church that had turned black along
with the neighborhood, but he was a national force among
ethnic minorities. He helped them muster their political voices
while tempering hostility about the black struggle for equality.
If my voice had counted, Monsignor Geno Baroni would have

been my run-away candidate for Pope. He was my personal icon whether he wore his starched collar or not. He not only was an important ghetto voice—a white man's voice—on the fractious stage of race relations, but he understood that the Catholic Church had to be on this frontier to stay true to the beliefs of both his black and sometimes reluctant, doubting white constituents. This challenging view spilled over onto other rigid Church doctrine, sometimes to the consternation of his Bishop.

It was because of his enthusiasm for bending rules that I was able to marry Louise under a semblance of the blessing of her faith. We were married at least in proximity of the altar of St. Francis church. Next door, in the rectory. It was a modest Judeo-Christian compromise that was enormously important to Louise. Her belief was more than a religious anchor, it mirrored who she was. She was one of three people I have known who illuminated their devotion to Christianity, not the other way around. The other two were Sargent Shriver and Rose Fitzgerald Kennedy.

The wedding site was no small matter, for both of us, for the Church, or, more significantly, for her emissary. Interfaith marriage was not often found, and certainly not blessed in the contemporary clerical rule book for Roman Catholic priests. That one party in the union was Jewish freighted the challenge. Ours may have been the only Catholic wedding ceremony ever held where Jesus Christ or any of his apostles never were mentioned. Not once.

Geno knew both of us. He knew me from our occasional work together on common poverty issues. He was among Sarge's drafted advisors. He knew Louise as a substitute teacher in one of Washington's toughest high schools. She had become a minor celebrity in the educational jungle of Washington's ghetto schools because she never had a ruckus in her class and never had to call the principal's office for assistance.

Edgar and Louise on their honeymoon.

Louise and I first met in what seemed like a scene pilfered from the pages of a pulp romance novel: a Vermont ski slope with the pulp-appropriate name, Magic Mountain. I was engaged in one of my periodic irrepressible outbursts of exhibitionism. I was yodeling on the chairlift. It was one of the last tailings of my Swiss heritage. Moments later she and her sister were in the lift line, a couple of skiers behind me. Her sister had connected the yodel with the yodeler. She pushed Louise forward until she was standing firmly on the back of my skis. It was an introductory maneuver hardly unique in the annals of ski slope pairings. Within moments we understood we had connections to Springfield. She was born there and I had put down some roots as a new landowner; working for the weekly, the *Springfield Reporter*.

We rode the lift together and the conversation never ended until that wind-chilled evening in December 1967 that brought my mother, Sarge, and Geno together in the discomfort of that intensive care room.

There is a puzzling aura that shrouds a serious accident. It contains the complexity and sometimes the hurt of the past with the creeping, emerging, fragile rebirth of the present. Like a chick squirming out of its shell, it's a struggle, a beginning. Each tentative movement is encased in its own challenges, vivid, daunting. A kind of step-after-step blueprint that replaces what was at birth natural, a reflex progression amid the remarkable mystery of becoming a person. These small scenes are unremembered by the principal actor in the drama. Who recalls the parental applause when you first crawled across the length of the living room floor? The first time you stood on your own feet, tottering precariously, balanced only by the security of a mother's hand? Who remembers those first tentative steps of walking?

But in that intensive care room, among the blinking machines, each of those calibrated indicators monitored a sliver of renewal. Each dial was an electronic messenger hiding a scary peak, a mountain range of personal adversaries to be conquered. The dials recorded progress, miniature bits, previously unnoticed, taken for granted. Like a laboratory slide that appears blank until it is magnified under the microscope. Suddenly it's alive with visible, moving shapes, twitching across that glass surface. That hospital room was my microscope, magnifying the smallest movements: my arm gingerly, in slow motion, reaching toward the stainless steel tray by my bed; trying to grasp the stainless steel bar above to help me move a couple inches to the side of the bed; hesitatingly reaching for the straw poking out of the glass so I could guide it to my mouth without the nurse's help.

In the guide book for recovery, the first underlined requirement is that you have to have the will to pull yourself out of the abyss. In the first weeks in intensive care I didn't have that will. I didn't want to focus on tomorrow. Not on any of the tomorrows. If I could have reached the tubes connecting me to the machines, I would have pulled them out. But I couldn't reach them.

The dictionary defines recovery as "to convey back as to a previous place or position... to restore..." But how do you do that? How do you do that when you're caught in the emotional whirlpool of descent?

It happens imperceptibly. A glimmer here, a glimmer there amid the dark shadows. It is among the most impenetrable mysteries of the human condition. Why does one person recover and another doesn't?

It is a collective response to the most crucial 911 call of your life. A sequence of kindnesses that come in the smallest packages: a nurse taking time to tell you about her children, details about her house at the end of a dirt road. She suddenly is more than a white-gowned professional bringing your medicine on the tray filled with small white paper cups. She becomes a real person. A recognizable person in the suddenly narrowed geography of your life.

It is a gradual build-up of generosity, like the many layers that eventually turn the irritant grain of sand of the oyster into a pearl. I don't pretend to understand it. But I know it appeared for me. A communal rallying, a series of singulars that make such a powerful plural in the life of another human being. I couldn't ignore it. I couldn't dismiss it.

There were phone calls that had to be rationed because they were so numerous. Every week a delegation of co-workers would make the 12 hour drive from Washington to appear at my bedside. Letters and cards—hundreds of them—that the nurses had to pile up in cardboard boxes around my bed. I have saved only one of those letters. It has hung on my library wall for more than 40 years. Like most of the other cards and letters it contained the overly generous phrases that are part of the ritual of condolence. For me the letter, like the boxes filled with others, contained the adrenalin for recovery.

> *I am surely not in the habit of writing anonymously, but you do not know me, nor I you. What I have to say is very personal so I will remain unknown. I write to bring courage to what must be a very difficult experience for you. I know of you through young people on this continent and others whose lives have been touched by yours. To them there has been no finer spirit in Washington than yours. They believe in our country, our government, and specifically in the Poverty program largely because of your idealism...Your return to your job will be a satisfaction to many as well as a challenge to you. I know specifically of prayers for your recovery from far corners of the world.*
>
> *Sincerely, An Unknown*

It was just a letter, now a bit faded. It was, however, a single, stemmed flower that combined with those hundreds of letters in the boxes by my bed to form the bouquet of renewal.

The letters, the phone calls, the visitors. They were a mosaic of generosity, of caring, that became the stimulus that lifted me out of the abyss.

It happened almost subconsciously, mysteriously. Gradually, after a month, I began to shed the past to focus on tomorrow. Yes, tomorrow when they would lift me out of that bed and into the wheelchair and navigate me to the Rehabilitation Unit. "Focus" is an inadequate word for the laser-like concentration it took even to attempt the most simple challenge. Trying to get up out of that wheelchair, even when assisted by the physical therapist. The parallel-bar railing of the 12 foot long walking track that, from my perspective, looked to be the length of the George Washington Bridge, maybe longer. The three-step incline that let me learn—again—how to climb stairs. They looked like a replica of Mount Everest. I can't do that! I can't! Each of them became the single-minded goal of my hospital day. I would think about them after they wheeled me back to my room, in the afternoon, in the early evening, parsing them into the tiniest component that I would attempt in the next day's session.

After a certain time the hospital room became my cocoon, my private, constricted world, comforting because of the certitude of its predictable daily rhythms. Waking up because a hand is on my wrist measuring my pulse rate, the day shift nurse recording on the clipboard the readings of the machinery around my bed, every morning, every day. The nurse's aide bringing a meal tray at the same appointed hour with the paper slip with my name on it, detailing the mimeographed checked boxes that told me what I could and couldn't eat. It was precise, clinically efficient right down to the exact number of ounces you could have of each offering.

It was a comfort. The repetitive, predictable check points of my day. After more than three months in that hospital, the room had become my village, a small enclave with each villager fulfilling a special role. The "mayor" was the ward supervisor who poked her head into the room, checked the charts at the foot of my bed, and left, generally with a nod and an encouraging phrase; the doctors were the presumed village elders, probably knowing that they ruled only with acquiescence of the nurses who followed their written orders.

But it was the villagers with the name tag "Practical Nurse" that were the most important citizens in my hamlet. They shared their own lives with me—the report card of their first grader, the foibles of a wandering husband. Most important of all, they were the dispensers of what to me were the Tiffany gift boxes of hospital life. The sure, professional hands of a back rub that became a totem of renewal; the fresh, newly ironed sheets that restored a disheveled bed.

Years later they would show up again on the radar screen of my life when I was chairman of the Vermont House of Representative's Health & Welfare Committee. The practical nurses were threatened with extinction, in part, by the zealotry of the high priests of academic nursing who intoned that the complexity of medical technology no longer made them relevant. These savants, it seemed, didn't know about the healing power of a practical nurse, about the practical parts of their medical ministry. Their willingness to listen to patients who needed to tell their stories so they could go on to the next chapter of their lives, their personal attention to patients.

Maybe they didn't know about the therapeutic gift of back rubs, or the restorative lift of a freshly made bed. My legislative Committee would not permit the closure of the last training school for practical nurses.

Like all villages, mine had a political system. This need became apparent and was emphasized after the nurses learned of my past enthusiasm in the political arena. I had been in my hospital village for so long that we were approaching the quadrennial March spectacle, the New Hampshire presidential primary. The powerful nurse constituency sprang to action: a write-in campaign for President for their favorite political patient.

Remarkably, I carried my ward, hospital ward that is. I received 7 votes for President of the United States. Unfortunately, these were tabulated under the catch-all category of "Other" so my ward victory remained anonymous. I was encouraged, however, by my tally. Particularly since it was achieved in a New Hampshire primary by a "candidate" who actually lived in Vermont and whose immigrant, naturalized citizenship collided head on with a constitutional requirement that you had to be native-born to be President.

My hospital confinement ended shortly afterwards with another visit from my friend Sarge. He carried a large laundry bag of books, an English–French dictionary and the paperback Berlitz volumes of "French Made Easy."

"Here," he said. "Start on these. We're going to Paris."

Days before, President Johnson relieved him from the increasingly contentious front lines of the War on Poverty and appointed him as his ambassador to France. I understood immediately the real meaning of "we're going to France." Sarge Shriver had the choice of hundreds of bright, fluent French speaking Foreign Service officers to help him. I was in a wheelchair and would have to wait at least until I graduated to crutches before I could even board the plane not to mention work daily in the Paris embassy.

The gesture was more than a gesture. I understood the message contained: it was a long-stemmed rose for the bouquet of my rehabilitation.

Edgar with Louise's sister, Maggie Lockridge, 2011.

With two of Maggie's granddaughters, about 2010.

Edgar with niece Michaela Bensko and her daughter.

With grand-niece Sophia Lockridge, 2007.

Maggie Lockridge and Edgar in 2007.

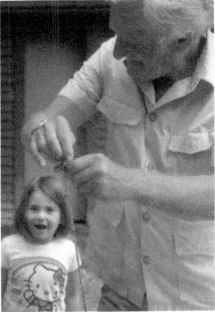

Teaching Rachael and Eli Kunkel how to bait a hook, and fish, at Muckross about 2010.

Dancing with Elena Schlossberg-Kunkel, 1999.

CHAPTER SEVEN

Île Saint-Louis

The stairway twisted and curled upwards in the eternal dusk of Paris entryways. It was anchored in time and place not only by the polished brass rods that held the worn but spotless carpet to each rising step, but by the air of permanence, of history, of a sheltered refuge, lightly perfumed by the musty odor that has lived comfortably in its shadows, lived there long before and after the footfalls of periodic French invaders on the cobblestone streets beyond its 16th century walls.

The stairway spoke to me in less hallowed and more ominous tones. It was supposed to be the gateway to my new apartment, perched like an eagle's nest, on the *cinquieme etage,* the walk up's fifth floor. I still needed a navigational aid of a single crutch, having recently graduated from a wheelchair. The climb looked Everestian.

"You can do it," said my friend, novelist James Jones, the author of the World War II classic, From Here to Eternity, who lived on the first two floors. "It will be good rehabilitation for you." Right! I reflected on that observation frequently throughout the coming months, usually gasping for breath at a landing between the higher floors.

That stairway became part of the continuum that began in that hospital rehabilitation unit, literally, step by step. But this time, the lesson was wrapped in the splendor of the "City of Lights." The apartment's terrace overlooked the bustling water highway that was the river Seine. At night it became a flickering, electric necklace, coal barges with their stream of blue running lights, yachts with their twinkling, illuminated masts and a parade of tourist boats whose battery of floodlights brought sweeping, explosive daylight to the walls of historic buildings on the river's bank. Including my bedroom, sometimes at the most inopportune moment.

The adjacent highway was a parallel strand. The flickering car headlights, the whoosh of a passing motor scooter weaving acrobatically between the lanes, the tour buses with their microphoned voices of guides extolling the historic wonders in multiple languages. And always, always, the swarm of horn-honking black box-shaped taxis that needed to sound their presence whether there was anything in front of them or not.

It was a feast. A multi-colored celebration of Gaelic life. It produced a new appreciation for my grandfather and his father who were able to call themselves Frenchmen. But with the warmth came the chill of a daily discomfort. The language. Or more precisely, the lack of it. The English–French dictionary and the first lesson plan Sarge Shriver had dumped on my hospital bed had their shortcomings.

"La plume de ma tante est sur le bureau de mon oncle," was the opening phrase that greeted me and a stream of Anglo-Saxons trying to master "Introductory French." While it told me that my aunt's pen was on my uncle's bureau, it had limited use in the streets and shops of Paris. Not to mention, in the subtle, nuanced linguistic complexity of French diplomacy.

That point was made only a few months after my arrival.

It was an embassy reception in the ornate, sprawling ambassadorial living room. The audience was an artful blend of government factotums and some of the venerated intelligentsia lured out of the intellectually-walled French universities. I was sitting next to Sarge trying to compose my facial expression to what I thought was the required thoughtfulness for the impeccable oration of one of our academic guests, when Sarge poked me.

"What's he saying? What's he saying?"

"How the hell do I know—I'm on the same lesson you're on!"

Gradually, sometimes snail-paced gradually, we both managed to overcome this handicap. That same ambassadorial living room turned out to be the venue of opportunity in locating my Île Saint-Louis apartment. It was at another reception that I met Jim and Gloria Jones.

Jim and his wife were the sole reason I had access to this special perch high on an island in the middle of the Seine. My balcony faced the Left Bank and gave me the chance to eavesdrop on French history. From the 12th century Notre Dame Cathedral, which took longer to build than the entire history of my country, to the Panthéon and Napoleon's tomb, directly in view, its dome bathed nightly in an incandescent swath that helped affirm the nickname "City of Lights."

The Jones' had put in a special word to the landlady, the former "special friend" of a French industrialist, who had bought the pied-a-terre for her after she may have tired of diamond necklaces and other doodads that are the time-honored currency of lovers. She apparently was a formidable student of what occasionally has been called an auxiliary French national sport: outwitting le Bureau des Impots, the tax department. She spurned a lease or any other written document that would confirm our mercantile relationship. Monthly rent payments had to be in cash delivered to her personally in a plain envelope with no hint of the identity of its recipient.

The Île Saint-Louis is a village in the middle of Paris. Before the creep of gentrification, its citizens only reluctantly accepted, and sometimes not at all, that the Ile was part of Paris and its sprawling, traffic-clogged metropolis. It was a real village, not only with its own zip code, but its own post office. It had its church, its village square, several bakeries—with the smell of fresh twice-a-day baked baguettes in the air—a hardware store, several florists, the best homemade ice cream shop in the city, innumerable restaurants, its own cheese store, branch bank and the essential anchor of French life itself, the neighborhood café.

The café was the wellspring of island news, more accurately translated: gossip. The impeccable source? The concierge. My English–French dictionary defined concierge as a "house porter, portress, door keeper." It was one of the most insufficient, understated translations in the entire volume. "La port-ress" not only guarded the door zealously, but protected some of the most intriguing snippets of Paris life. And no one knew them better than Madame la Concierge. Her fidelity to silence outside of her professional inner circle was not only a conci-erge code of honor, but was a direct link to the content of the annual envelope that materially brightened her holiday season.

A squadron of these concierge guardians met every morn-ing for the anticipated news exchange, lubricated with "un rouge," the fueling that was the day's first glass of red wine. The agenda has remained unaltered in unspoken reverence to the historical continuity that our island required. The comings and goings of the village inhabitants were dissected in the most enticing detail, in a blend of factual and embellished tales of nocturnal activities, punctuated with knowing nods or a wink of the eye. When the morning reports were completed and the glasses empty, each would repair to their natural habi-tat. More often than not, it was a cubbyhole of an apartment facing the main entrance door so she could interrogate every stranger. In her shadowed lair, she usually wore the traditional uniform of her trade—bedroom slippers and a one-size-too-large wool bathrobe, wrapped securely under a large protec-tive apron. It was a sartorial portrait that would remain un-changed for most of the day.

The concierge network, meeting every morning in the corner café, was a tradition as predictable as the hourly tolling of the island's church bell. This small hamlet concept was not a romantic invention of wishful reverie. It was a Gaelic reality. A village can exist in the middle of urban hurly burly, a certi-tude as clear as its unstated air of superiority over those ordinary folk—no matter how high to the manor born—who had the misfortune of calling home some other place than their island in the middle of a river in Paris.

"Ah, Je suis désolé,"–*I am sorry*–the island's hardware store proprietor told me one afternoon after rummaging through aged drawers looking for a special hinge I needed. "Vous devez aller à Paris pour ça." *You have to go to Paris for that.*

On another occasion when I arrived near closing time at the neighborhood bakery to buy that afternoon's baguette, I was reminded of the lateness of the hour and the clearly regretful suggestion: "Monsieur May, Je regrette, Je n'ai plus, vous devez allez au continent." *I'm sorry, I don't have anymore, you have to go to the continent.*

There was that soothing comfort of belonging, of being part of a place, a community of souls bound together by a special neighborhood they could call their own. The Île Saint-Louis was a place where you were recognized as an individual in the sea of anonymity that washes over urban life.

"Ah, Bonjour, Monsieur May," the horse meat lady would greet me as I passed her slit of a store whose entrance was adorned by an enormous carved equine head. It was a time when her specialty cuts still found a place at many neighborhood dinner tables. Like other island merchants, she would proffer a forgiving smile in response to my occasional inventive French phrases, salted now and then with a desperate word of fractured Franglais. Sometimes, she would gently pick up a dangling participle or an errant tense and offer a soft correction.

As in all French villages, the daily commerce was focused on the corner post of French values: food, artfully displayed, often squeezed, sniffed and consistently compared to last week's offering. On a particularly slow day, the daily ceremony would reach further back in history, perfumed with nostalgia, to a more complex, pre-World War II era that always found today's display—regretfully—wanting. Assisted by the inherited gene pool of my French grandfather, I absorbed this ritual effortlessly.

I started every daily gastronomic voyage at the source: cheese at the fromagerie; meat at the boucherie; baguettes, pastries and cakes at the boulangerie; and wine, of course wine, at Chez Nicolas, le magasin de vin. These were mandatory daily habits, as common as an Englishman taking an umbrella when he leaves his house, regardless of the weather report. One is comforted by these certainties of daily life.

I was uplifted by the visual portraits freshly painted every morning, by the store owners displaying their wares. A leg of lamb—butterflied and bound with butcher's twine and adorned with strategically dotted sprigs of parsley—fresh killed chicken with plucked necks and feathered heads intact, symmetrically lined up on overhead hooks like troops readying for inspection. At the cheese store, the Boursault formed a circle on top of a fan of autumn leaves, carefully arranged not to intrude on its Camembert neighbors.

At the fruit and vegetable store, each fruit had its own role in the architectural design, displayed in a pyramid of plentitude that showed each pear, each peach, each apple with its best face jutting outward. Almost daily I exchanged greetings with Madame who presided over this colorful tableau.

"Deux poires, s'il vous plaît," I would request after the preliminary cordialities. *Two pears, please.*

"Pour cette soirée?"–*For this evening?*–she asked.

"Oui, Madame."

She climbed a rickety stepladder and reached for the pears. She fingered several, moving carefully from one to the other. She removed the third pear, sniffed it, nodded almost imperceptibly, and returned her fingers to the pyramid, in search of that second ripe pear for this evening.

"Voila!" she said, with a trace of a smile, punctuating the completion of a personal goal.

If the daily rhythm of Île Saint-Louis' narrow streets was a microcosm of French village life, the island's two-story home of James and Gloria Jones was the artistic salon of the Paris expatriates. Chez Jones was the outpost that had become the successor to Sylvia Beach's bookstore, Shakespeare & Co. In the Twenties the store had been the Left Bank debating center for a roster of global wanderers that included Ernest Hemingway and Gertrude Stein.

More than thirty years later a similar literary convocation had moved upstream along the Seine and skipped over the bridge to the Île Saint-Louis, to Jim and Gloria Jones' emporium. Among its denizens were some of the post-World War luminaries of American letters, including Irwin Shaw, William Styron, and an occasional visit of Mary McCarthy who lived in Paris. Sometimes these gatherings were spiced by a stormy pop-in from James Baldwin, the short, near frail, talented writer whose residential anchor was in southern France, allowing a periodic pit stop in Paris.

One of the more turbulent Baldwin visits featured an un-planned added attraction: the gendarmes who came uninvited to a post-midnight party. "Les flics" (French argot for "the cops") crashed the event after the guests' generous consump-tion of spirits had clearly outdistanced their spirited discus-sion. Sometime after midnight the volume-enhanced debate had moved to the narrow, darkened street below. The leading and most vocal voices were Jim Jones and James Baldwin. At the conclusion of a particularly vociferous debate, Jones, who that night had tumbled off his physician-prescribed wagon, took umbrage at Baldwin calling his host a "honkey mother f-----." Jones promptly ejected Baldwin from his digs and, just for emphasis, chased him down the darkened street. The top-of-the-lungs Jones' response referred ungraciously to Baldwin's blackness, not to mention his sexual orientation. It was an Anglo-Saxon summary unsuitable for children's ears but with sufficient volume to wake the neighbors. Enter "les flics." As a self-appointed peacemaker, I tried to explain. "Vous savez,"– *You know*–I appealed to the officers, "ils sont les écrivains amé-ricains. Ils sont tous un peu fou." *They're American writers, they're all a little crazy.*

"Oui" came the confirmation with what I thought was a sympathetic edge. It was accompanied by an easily translatable suggestion that the debate should return behind the thick walls where the alcohol-infused commentary might be a bit shielded from the neighbors.

During many nights, this enthusiastic literary colony in-cluded Jim's close friend, Irwin Shaw, author of The Young Lions, another of the World War II star novels. While he lived in the Swiss ski resort of Klosters, Irwin had a pied-àterre in Paris that brought him around frequently. Our three-some occasionally convened for a multi-hour, wine-marinated lunch in a Left Bank bistro that not only was anchored in gastronomic excellence, but was energized by free form debates that could span the latest political or literary gossip. These were usually accompanied by imaginative, wishful speculation about the nocturnal activities of the all-curves-in-the-right-places barmaid refilling our glasses.

Adam Kunin with Edgar at the Eiger, around 2000.

Cross-country skiing at Muckross, 2006.

Irwin surprised both Jim and Gloria Jones when he volunteered to coax me back on skis, something the post-accident orthopedists said would not happen. Irwin Shaw skied with the same hell-bent-for-leather brio as he wrote novels. He applied one simple geometric truism to the sport. The shortest distance between two points is a straight line. Even if the geography happened to be an Alpine peak. When he coaxed me down the beginners slope in Klosters, not once but a number of times, the scene appeared so out of character that there were camera clicks to verify it.

Irwin was one of the regulars at the James Jones symposiums where no topic—literary, political or artfully risqué—was ruled out of order. The weekly catalyst, however, was less intellectual and more pragmatic. The Sunday night poker game always was accompanied by Gloria's celebrated spaghetti dinner with a sauce she claimed was perfected by generations of cooks in her Italian-rooted family.

Sunday night poker at Gloria and Jim's for these expatriates was not for the faint of heart. You better be as good at cards as your imagination believed to be at love, only slightly less adept than the talents of Minnesota Fats in the first, and Rudolf Valentino, in the second. During my first and last exposure at the card table I lost at least half of my weekly pay. For some of us those Sunday nights were far safer as a spectator sport.

Among the more significant world events in our Paris years was the summer night when Neil Armstrong stepped out of his space capsule onto the moon. My terrace, overlooking the Seine, clearly was the venue of choice. Our island neighbor, the talented film director John Frankenheimer, couldn't have ordered a more dramatic stage. It was a full-moon night in Paris. The yellow sphere hung in front of us like a back-lighted, giant pumpkin above the Panthéon. The television set, temporarily installed on the terrace, zoomed in on Armstrong about to descend the spacecraft ladder. An hour earlier one of my French friends had brought special gifts to mark the occasion. I asked him what was in the bulging paper bags.

"Ah, quelques mortier," he said.

"Mortars! What are you going to do with mortars in the middle of Paris?"

He explained, while planting the slender mortar tubes in the balcony's flower boxes. This was such a historic occasion that it required more than a handful of celebratory fire crackers. Before I could ask what was in the second bag, he unwrapped a half-dozen projectiles, accompanied with a magician's wave, "Voila."

On the balcony of the Île Saint-Louis apartment, about 1970.

Less than a minute after Armstrong's foot stirred the first man-made cloud of dust on the moon, the No. 1 shell zoomed out of the flower box with a trailing hiss, rising above the Seine, and burst into a sparkling umbrella of multi-colored stars. The second shell brought Left Bank traffic to a halt. The third moved diners in the three-star Tour d'Argent across the river to the floor-to-ceiling windows to watch the pyrotechnics. The fourth was aborted because of an energetic knock on the apartment door.

Once more: "les flics." This time they were a little breathless from their speedy five floor ascent. But they left little doubt that the sparkling drama had come to an end. The uniformed trio, with their badges of authority gleaming, listened courteously as my French friends told them, with arm-flailing emphasis, that it was imperative to celebrate dramatically such a dramatic event. I thought I detected several law-and-order nods of appreciation of the historic import of the occasion, even if it was made-in-America historic. Each gendarme was handed a glass, and we joined in a chorus toast to Neil Armstrong and the "one step for mankind" that had just taken place.

In parting, they saluted as they returned to the winding stairway, suggesting, by the way, that we might want to save the rest of our ammunition for a more bucolic celebration in the countryside. That event, for me, may have been the zenith of Franco-American relations in our Paris years.

That diplomatic objective, incidentally, was no small matter in our Paris assignment. In addition to a new language, I soon learned that the diplomatic seismograph was among the most sensitive instruments known to humankind. It detected the slightest of tremors, registered nuances, implications, and, occasionally, offered a tiny kernel of importance wrapped artfully in a convoluted sentence. Sarge Shriver was one of those gifted people who instinctively could untangle obscure phrases and find that grain of meaning—even when it was encased in formal diplomatic French, crafted by the equally formal embassy translator. When we first arrived in France, the phrase, "constructive dialogue" may have been diplomatically appropriate to describe conversations between our countries, but the clarity surrounding the word "chill" was more truthful, if not sufficiently diplomatic.

General Charles de Gaulle had evicted American-dominated NATO out of Paris with the conviction that he would rebuild the grandeur of Napoleonic France without any—thank you very much—help from the Americans. The expulsion order, some were convinced, also contained the backwash of a bruised ego whose owner was still smarting about the perceived slights from when he was a member, if not a sufficiently honored member, of the triumvirate of the World War II Allied command.

Ambassador Shriver, reenergized from the poverty wars, would no more accept this hardening of diplomatic arteries than acquiesce to the heresy that Franco-American friendship, born in the American Revolution, was not susceptible to improvement—a Kennedy/Shriveresque conviction that recognized no international barriers.

Sometimes it resembled the intensity of the 1960 Presidential campaign. Shriver barnstormed not only in the cities, but the French countryside, whenever an invitation was extended. From the apple-scented hills that produced the brandies of Normandy to the internationally venerated vineyards of Bordeux to the pre-dawn visit to the Marseilles wholesale fish market where hefty lady fish mongers welcomed him with gap-toothed smiles and wraparound hugs, whose enthusiastic embrace, at least for the moment, obliterated their loyal Communist Party voting record.

Sarge had a joie de vie, a joy of life, that his audiences seemed to relish even if they had some difficulty deciphering his occasional Franglais-flavored discourse. Sometimes he was a tad ahead or a smidgen behind his lofty translated-into-French phrases. In Normandy, one afternoon, we celebrated what appeared to me to be the never-ending anniversary of one more World War II liberated French town. After a festive five-course meal, Sarge concluded the event with a diplomatic American response and an enthusiastic closing toast.

"Je veux lever mon verre... "–*I want to raise my glass*– he read the sometimes phonetically spelled out French text, and then suddenly realized that the glass in question still was firmly rooted on the white, starched tablecloth in front of him. A pause, a slight smile that spoke more of amusement than of embarrassment, and an inquiry: "... Où est mon verre?"–*where is my glass?*–the applause reverberated around the room, accompanied by a flurry of fingers pointing to the anchored crystal.

I thought then that the Ambassador of the United States of America had a better chance of winning an election to the French Chamber of Deputies, than for governor of his native Maryland. That turned into something more than fanciful conjecture when a later Maryland political foray was considered and was rejected. But the diplomatic climate change in the Shriver years was more than an irrepressible, ever optimistic American ambassador. It was a mainstay of the family business.

Eunice Kennedy Shriver was in no danger of being mistaken for a demure backstage spouse who rearranged the Residence's furniture and periodically sponsored an art show or a visiting American string quartet. She was a force, a weather system of her own and, once formed, could neither be diminished nor diverted. She was aided by two realities. First, the affection the French had for her brother, President Kennedy, who won Parisian hearts when, at the end of their first state visit he described himself as "the man who accompanied Jacqueline Kennedy to Paris—and I have enjoyed it."

Secondly, Eunice was determined to ignore the sometimes frigid diplomatic breezes and launch a Special Olympics program in France, where the mentally challenged were often hidden from public view by self-conscious parents. Among those parents were President and Madame Charles de Gaulle. They had an afflicted daughter who was kept in the silent shadows.

De Gaulle ordered the elite national Institut des Sports, the training powerhouse of French athletes and coaches in suburban Vincennes, to assist her in launching a French chapter of Special Olympics. Sarge asked me to help on the very optimistic assumption that my embryonic French linguistic skills would underpin Eunie's machine gun fire Franglais that sometimes perplexed both American and French listeners.

In spite of the linguistic hurdles, a year later the French Special Olympics existed with its own national games. Shortly afterwards, a French team was the first international entry in the U.S. games in Chicago to be followed in future years by teams from 182 countries. Second only to the quadrennial Olympics themselves, these Special Olympic International games were to become the largest global sporting event.

After the 1968 Presidential election results were tallied—
with Richard Nixon narrowly defeating Hubert Humphrey—
our diplomatic life expectancy drastically shortened. Sarge,
like all Presidential appointees, submitted the expected formal
resignation. Every day we sifted through the diplomatic pouch
for the anticipated White House eviction notice. Silence.

The message that did arrive in the Embassy Communica-
tions center announced that one of the first international visits of the new President would be to France to meet personally
with President de Gaulle. Beside the sudden arrival of a phalanx of White House staff and Secret Service agents, the visit
had its special dramatic components—the ambassadorial couple who would host the Presidential visit had worked strenu-
ously and successfully to keep Nixon from that job eight years
earlier. It was no small challenge in the annals of political eti-
quette.

Like virtually every Kennedy family nesting place, the residence of the American Ambassador at 2 Avenue d'Iéna was a
mini museum of Kennedy family political history—from Rose
Fitzgerald Kennedy's father, "Honey" Fitz, the mayor of Boston to her husband, Joseph P. Kennedy, President Roosevelt's
ambassador to Great Britain; to his son, the President of the
United States. Every lace doily-covered side table and book-
shelf contained family photographs of Kennedy outings from
foreign safaris to sun splashed sailings in Hyannis Port, framed
Presidential letters, snippets of personal notes, including President Kennedy's handwritten jottings from the Cuban Missile
Crisis. I remember when we first escorted the head of the
presidential advance team through the residence, where Presi-

dent Nixon would hold his reciprocal diplomatic dinner. He paused, momentarily, in front of each of these shrines to the past. We didn't need words to comprehend the message. Most, but not all of these historical markers, were temporarily removed.

What surprised me most, however, was that the cargo plane preceding the Presidential visit not only contained the armored limousine with its Presidential seal, but a complete White House dinner service including the food that would appear on those plates. Among the squadron of temporary personnel were the White House cooks who would prepare the meal.

This was a gastronomic coals-to-Newcastle tremor that shook not only our resident chef but, I suspected, rattled the acres of Victorian iron framework of Les Halles, the renowned Paris wholesale food market—not to mention the culinary high priests ensconced in the Michelin *Red Guide*. It was particularly puzzling since the resident chef, like the embassy furniture, was part of the inheritance of succeeding ambassadors. Our chef was not just another cook, but had developed a star reputation. One of the highlights of my Paris tenure was his friendship and his periodic invitation to share a particular gastronomic creation in his personal dining alcove off the kitchen.

The state dinner, however, even in the critical French press, was appraised as a diplomatic success. Some days later it was followed by an appreciative note from the President. The second significant encounter with the White House ended on a lesser note.

We were fired.

It began with a phone call from President Nixon. He called
with an offer. He wanted to appoint Shriver as Ambassador to
the United Nations. Sarge apparently had turned from an earlier election adversary into an asset—the possibility of Nixon
touting a Kennedy, albeit an in-law, appealed to his administration.

Sarge and Edgar, early 1990s.

The offer was made personally by the President. It was followed by telephonic strategy sessions with several of Sarge's
closest Peace Corps confidants, Bill Moyers and Harris Wof-
ford, subsequently a United States Senator from Pennsylvania.
After all our back and forths Shriver told the President that he
was honored by the offer, but he could not accept it.

Within a week our replacement in Paris was named. It was
time to pack. I remember the airport departure. We were in
the VIP lounge at Charles de Gaulle Airport, a sheltered, ele-
gantly furnished enclave for arriving and departing dignitar-
ies. We were a mélange of embassy senior staff, a smattering
of French officialdom, and a few close friends.

The tinkle of champagne glasses with their farewell toasts were interrupted by the arrival of a tall impeccably uniformed French military officer. He was President de Gaulle's personal military aide. He carried a huge bouquet of roses that, with a slight bow and a gloved salute, he proffered to Eunice. The compliments of the President of France. A personal note to one of his favorite Americans was discreetly fastened to the wrapping.

Sarge, unidentified man, Edgar, Arnold Schwarzenegger, early 1990s.

I stayed at the airport until the wheels of the airliner lifted off the runway. The ambassadorial limousine brought me back to the Embassy. The driver parked it in its usual premier space and to my surprise, shook my hand, knuckle-squeezing firmly, in what was a moment of farewell.

I mounted the marble stairway to my office and saw that the cables to my power source had been disconnected. A crew was packing my personal papers and books into cardboard boxes that were already cluttering the carpeted hallway.

My own role in all of these adventures was small. It was, at best, a minimalist performance on the periphery of Franco-American diplomacy. I wrote speeches for Sarge who delivered them with junior varsity gusto at the never ending Normandy landing celebrations; at solemn memorials in American military cemeteries where the snap of windswept flags disturbed the hushed reverence that lived among vast fields of geometric patterns of white crosses; and in the cobble-stoned village squares where a mayor would recall the arrival of mudsplattered American tanks, followed by a single file of G.I.s liberating his village.

Eunice and Edgar, working on Special Olympics project.

Amid these totems of history, the flurry of embassy dinners, the white-gloved servers at diplomatic receptions, the nightly illumination of the "City of Lights," I understood my role. It was more personal than diplomatic. Maybe it was not my role at all that was particularly relevant. Maybe it was Sarge Shriver's self-assigned task: to challenge, prod, encourage me to rebuild my life.

With Sarge after a fishing trip (unidentified man at left), 1972.

CHAPTER EIGHT

M. l'Abbé

The ceiling of the 16th century church perched on the Mediterranean hills of southern France included a section that had been carefully and lovingly repaired. The restoration was a memory tug of days of violence that liberated this sunbaked cluster of walled hill towns in the waning days of World War II.

The restored section, like a fading water stain, became a personal burden for me, a plaster mixture of guilt by association. I had been in that church many times, accompanying my friend, the village priest, as he prepared for a daily Mass or a special service for the recently departed or the newly arrived.

Monsieur l'Abbé Pierre Beal was as much a fixture in Montauroux for its 932 inhabitants as was the one village café, the one central war monument to the dead of two World Wars, or the one cemetery with its fading flower bouquets marking weathered gravestones of those who for centuries had made life's journey from the village to the permanent place beneath the rocky soil on the village fringe.

As in many communities in southern France at the time, its popular mayor was elected on the Communist Party ticket. But unlike some other jurisdictions, the village priest and the communist mayor had worked out a respectful détente, an unwritten power sharing between the civil and the religious with neither trampling on the other's turf.

When Monsieur l'Abbé needed something from the village government, he saw the mayor who would quietly make it happen. When Monsieur le Maire needed a special prayer for an aging relative who still was a believer, the priest provided the blessing.

"C'est comme ça,"–*It's like that*–the villagers murmured approvingly.

Monsieur l'Abbé, in his sixties, always was dressed in an ankle length black cassock and black beret when in the narrow village streets, regardless of the sun splashed season. (Never mind that he wore shorts underneath to defend against the summer heat.)

The village priest was greeted with a "Bonjour, l'Abbé" and a deferential nod by every passerby, believers and non-believers alike. The latter appeared to be an expanding cohort as daily Mass sometimes dwindled to a smattering of black clad, white haired women whose gnarled fingers held the biography of thousands of family meal preparations, and the centuries old annual grape harvest that reached back to the days when the Romans tended the surrounding vineyards.

For M. l'Abbé, the declining flow of ritual worshipers was a minor but probably inwardly painful irritant in the continuum of baptisms, weddings and funerals for which he was the Bishop's latest master of ceremonies.

Our friendship was particularly meaningful to me.

Less than 50 miles away, the port city of Nice was an emotional touchstone in our family history. We had an uncle, aunt and a cousin there before the war. The cousin, a French soldier who was a prisoner of war, was repatriated months after France surrendered to the Germans. He was the last male to carry my mother's family name. The year after he returned to Nice, a neighbor turned him into the occupying Germans because his family was Jewish. He and his parents and the family name perished in the gas chambers of Hitler's fanaticism.

I came to this hill perched village because the priest's housekeeper was the mother of my friend, Pierre Carrere. I had worked with Pierre at the American Embassy in Paris. During an approaching Christmas holiday Pierre had invited me to the family homestead in the hills of Provence.

Pierre's mother, the housekeeper/cook, was a phenomenon. She produced Michelin Guide quality five course meals on a two-burner hotplate installed in the thick-walled rectory kitchen. She trundled each creation out—one spectacular course at a time—conscious of the daily Mediterranean rhythm that was dictated by the noonday heat. We convened around the outdoor tree-shaded dining table in a midday gastronomic tradition that was rooted long, long ago. Monsieur l'Abbé raised the meal's first (but not last) glass of wine with thanks to the bounty of the Lord's gifts, and to each of our well-being.

Madame Carrere accepted the oohs and aahs that followed the first tasting with the matter-of-fact elegance of a Parisian three star chef. She absorbed them with an appreciative diplomatic nod, knowing full well that her priest might be in charge at the church altar, but at the rectory there was only one high factotum, and this one wore an apron and a skirt.

Through the years, I was adopted into the family as the "le cousin d'Amerique," the American cousin, an affection-filled friendship that has continued, uninterrupted by either time or the span of continents that separated us.

Enjoying a meal with Monsieur l'Abbé.

On those frequent walks from the rectory to the church, as we entered the sanctuary, Monsieur l'Abbé always would provide a gentle reminder of my complicity, as an American, in the war drama that scarred his church. It was as constant as the confessional booth in the corner. And the connection between the booth and me did not need to be spoken.

"Tu vois," *You see,* he would say, *it's your compatriots who did that.* "Oui les Américains." There was a pointed finger to the blemish on the ceiling and the repeated, and repeated tale of how it happened.

It was a month after the Normandy invasion of France—the American and British armies had opened a second front on the beaches of southern France. The German army retreated from the coastal cities and towns but decided to make a stand in several of the walled villages on inland hills originally fortified by the Roman legions.

The Germans rained cannon fire on the approaching armies and they responded with mortar shells at the enemy holed up in the hilltop villages.

"Horreur!"

An errant shell landed on the church roof, opened a jagged splintered gap, and worse, much worse, seriously damaged the antique organ beneath. To M. l'Abbé, who welcomed the allied liberation, this was the greatest sin of all—silencing his beloved antique pipe organ whose resonating gold cylinders reached high above the altar.

For M. l'Abbé the rituals of ministering his priestly duties was a covenant with God, but music—making it, singing it, playing it—was a personal ecstasy that soared above the daily religious commandments into higher celestial terrain.

The errant mortar shell was more than a missile gone astray. It was a daily reminder of what today's latter day wars euphemistically describe as "collateral damage" that had abruptly silenced his precious organ. Because of a persistently modest Sunday collection plate, there never were enough coins or, for that matter, folded currency to make the major repairs. The instrument remained mute, polished weekly like a precious family heirloom... Until...

During the late sixties and early seventies of our Paris years, there was a constant turn-style slew of visitors to the residence of Ambassador Sargent and Eunice Kennedy Shriver. It reflected the diverse tableau of America—there were headline-making authors, musicians, diplomats, basketball players, politicians, tennis stars, opera singers, industrial titans and, that constantly expanding constituency, the Kennedy family kinfolk.

None, however, stirred the embassy's French and American staff more than "Madame Kennedy." This was *The* Madame Kennedy, the matriarch.

Rose Fitzgerald Kennedy held the maternal baton over what might have been the most determined group of overachiever offspring in American history. And it lasted a lifetime, held in place without ever a raised voice, but as a gentle anchor during whatever storm might hit a family member.

The occasional designer suit notwithstanding, she was consistently wrapped in a garment of serenity. It may have come from the adversity no normal human being should bear, or the strength of her faith that brought rewarding inner warmth from the daily Mass she attended. Whatever its source, it radiated from her whether she was in a Paris boutique, at a diplomatic dinner or reading a children's book to one of her legion of grandchildren.

Grandma, as she was called in the family lexicon of cherished titles, would come to Paris at least once a year to visit her daughter Eunice and her Ambassador son-in-law and, of course, go shopping. Generally around Christmas time.

In several of those years, Eunice, an avid skier, was off part of the time on some Alpine slope, leaving Sarge Shriver and me to entertain Grandma. It was hardly a hardship assignment for either of us.

Whether at some Michelin-starred restaurant or at the Opera, there always was a flurry of excitement wherever Madame Kennedy appeared. The maître de or store manager would recognize her instantly, much to her puzzlement. She was perplexed why anyone would want to make such a fuss over her, genuinely unaware that she was, for millions, a premier global heroine.

One evening the three of us were a minute late arriving at the Paris Opera. As we waited for the first scene to conclude with other latecomers, the general manager spotted us in the lobby. He was brought out of the theater by a ruckus caused by a well-known Parisian count who accused the Opera House of having set their clocks fast and starting the performance too early. After somewhat calming the count for his noisy protest, the manager scurried over to us.

"Ah, Madame Kennedy, Monsieur l' Ambassadeur, you can't be kept waiting here. S'il vous plaît, *please,* follow me." He led us to an inner corridor, opened a hidden doorway, and led us up a narrow circular stairway where he pulled back the velvet curtain of General de Gaulle's Presidential Box. "Voila!" he said.

A few minutes later Grandma leaned over to me and whispered, "You know, usually they only let very important people sit here."

The largest German television network found out about one of her Paris visits and called asking about an interview.

Sarge asked me to see if Grandma wanted to do it and, if af-firmative, negotiate with the German network on time and place and stick with her until the task was completed.

The answer was yes. The German producer brought his news anchor and crew to the residence where we filmed the interview. Rose Kennedy didn't need any coaching. She an-swered questions with charm and ease about her life as the matriarch of this Camelot family. Whenever the red light of the recording camera went on, it managed to absorb the se-renity that shrouded her. It didn't require an English–German translation for her large subsequent television audience to feel it.

After the interview the cameramen and their assistants, no strangers to international headliners, crowded around her waiting to be introduced. She had a question about their fami-lies and a phrase of thanks for each of them.

The producer pulled me aside and asked, "Where would you like us to send the honorarium?"

"The honorarium? What honorarium?"

"Well," he said, "when we interview someone of Mrs. Kennedy's stature, we offer an honorarium to a charity desig-nated by the interviewee."

Trying to rise to the expected diplomatic level of cool in matters about money and its quantity, I responded in a near whisper, "The honorarium? Can you give me some idea of what we are talking about?"

"Ten thousand mark, that's what we provide in special sit-uations like this."

I tried very hard to camouflage my body language as I heard the amount for a 45 minute interview. I'm not sure I succeeded.

"I will ask Mrs. Kennedy and get back to you."

They want to give you a 10,000 mark honorarium for the interview for one of your charities, I told her. Even Grandma seemed impressed by the amount.

"What do you think we ought to do with it?" she asked me.

"Why don't we think about it overnight and let's decide tomorrow."

In the pre-dawn hours of the morning, when semi-conscious thoughts flit across your mind's screen only to disappear when you wake up, there were images of Monsieur l'Abbé in the church, a spear-like finger pointing to an off-color splotch of ceiling, an antique pipe organ silent in its polished splendor...

This time, I remembered when I woke up.

"I think I have an idea about what you might want to do with the honorarium." I said.

I told her the complete story. She smiled when I spoke about my priest friend putting the pressure on this immigrant who escaped German persecution, finding a safe haven in his adopted country... about the American army chasing the occupiers out of the shimmering hills above the Mediterranean and the errant mortar shell that silenced the M. l'Abbé's precious instrument.

"That's a wonderful place for the honorarium," Grandma said. In an I-can't-help-it spontaneous reflex, I jumped up and gave her a hug. "Thank you."

Today, attached to the massive wall of a 16th century church built upon remains of an ancient Roman village perched high above the terraced vineyards, there is a brass plaque near the restored pipe organ.

"Grâce à Mme Rose Kennedy..." *Because of Rose Kennedy this war damaged organ was restored...*

This Sunday, like every Sunday in the intervening years, I imagine that the deep-throated sounds of the organ, directed by the successor to my departed friend, Monsieur l'Abbé, will ring out of the church. The resonating chords momentarily will strain against the confinement of the thick church walls and escape, joyously, wafting over the summer fields of blooming lavender, the scented air of wild thyme and rosemary, then soaring over the silver green olive trees and the spring built by the Romans... and gently lose themselves in the canopied azure sky of Provence.

CHAPTER NINE

Wedding

The leather bound book, with its cover of spider web cracks, spoke of history before it was even opened. Within its lined pages was the comforting chronology of essential village life. Names and dates, inscribed in the formal, precise, penmanship that gives municipal authority to the record of births, deaths, and marriages in the walled Mediterranean village perched high on a rocky hill overlooking a distant sea.

"History," in the village of Mons, incidentally, means a backward reach to the 11th century when villagers tended the vineyards and olive groves whose offspring still cling to the hillsides.

My interest in this registry of village life was focused, passionately, on a single category: the pages that recorded government sanctioned romance, Le Registre de Mariage. The earliest names in this accounting of the smitten appeared Au-

gust 14, 1844, one hundred and forty-three years before the
pages affirmed that on June 30, 1972...

> Mademoiselle Judith A. Hill, of Cuyahoga Falls, Ohio;
> Monsieur Edgar May, born in Zurich, Switzerland were
> married by his honor, Monsieur le Maire, Pierre Audibert.

Both the date and Judith's birthplace, it turned out, were
more than mundane legal markers along this lavender-
perfumed roadway to matrimony. Each of them brought the
wedding ceremony to a halt. The very first sentence not only
produced a pause, but initiated a decibel rising debate to which
most of the wedding guests made vocal, very vocal, contribu-
tions.

In France, in every city or village, the ceremony that cele-
brates the hoped-for permanence of romance may resonate
before a higher authority when guided by a priest, reverend,
rabbi or imam, but without the official municipal blessing
(and required legal text), solemnly pronounced by His Honor
the Mayor, the route to that registry of marriage is barred.
Fermez. *Closed.*

No one understood the import of this better than Mayor
Pierre Audibert. In his best black suit, emblazoned with the
large blue, white and red sash slanting across his chest—the
time honored badge of municipal office—he and his constituents clearly comprehended who the law put in charge of dura-
ble matters of the heart: Monsieur le Maire, Pierre Audibert.

To ensure the proper order of the trust conferred on him,
the mayor personally supervised the pre-nuptial preparation.
This began with the placement of chairs in the thick-walled
town hall, especially the exact location of two, directly in front

of his lectern—the place of honor for the two principals in the ritual. For the occasion, he brought a large vase of wild flowers that he placed on a doily-covered side table next to the lectern. He arranged them so that the most promising blossoms would face his audience.

In Mons, (pop. 254), marriages are not among the monthly calendared events. Ours was only the second of the year. Not only were the starring actors foreign, but this one had at least one accoutrement that I thought created some pulse-racing unease for the mayor. It was rumored that the former American Ambassador to France, a friend of the groom, would make a special trip to attend.

"The mayor," the bride-to-be observed, "looks a little bit nervous."

It was a perceptive observation.

"Bonjour, mes amis," the mayor said, tapping the lectern to quiet the ebullient audience while smiling at Judith and me, anchored directly in front of him. "We are here today...FILL IN THE BLANK..." he paused, "... the 31st day of June for the marriage of—" There was an immediate murmur from the assembled. Before the first official paragraph could be punctuated, the proceedings uniting Mademoiselle Hill of Cuyahoga Falls, Ohio and Monsieur May, born in Zurich, Switzerland were skittering down the vineyard lined hillside.

"Eh, Eh, Monsieur le Maire," one of the wedding guests shouted with arm-waving emphasis, "Si, aujourd'hui..."–*if today is the 31st of June this marriage is worth zero*–a mathematical sum that is an identical measurement whether you pronounce it in English or French.

"Monsieur," the mayor replied, puffing out his tri-color sash to its limits, "I didn't say today was the 31st, I said it was the *30th* of June."

"No, No, No," responded the wedding guest chorus, launching such a vigorous protest that it would have garnered applause from the galleries of the French version of Congress, the National Assembly in Paris. A few moments later a compromise was reached; Monsieur le Mayor would start again, from the beginning.

Unfortunately, the next linguistic roadblock was less one of content and more of pronunciation. "Cuyahoga Falls," was the precipice.

"Kee... Kei..." the mayor repeatedly attacked the American Indian name looking directly and, I thought, imploringly, at Judith.

"Cuyahoga Falls," his rescuer pronounced with the emphasis of a bride trying to stabilize a listing matrimonial ship.

"Oui!" the mayor said with an appreciative nod. And moved on.

Judith and I first met in one of the more mundane surroundings in Paris, in the United States Embassy cafeteria, an American satellite eatery determined to replicate the comfort of back home cuisine. Hamburgers with a companion of dill pickle, or for early morning openers, scrambled eggs with a side of fried potatoes. The scene reminded me of those first days in the gleaming Automats of many years ago. Only the "click, click" of coins was missing.

Our meeting took place at a less than optimum time of day. At breakfast when the fires of romance generally are banked or doused by some disastrous gaffe the night before. Apparently neither the site nor the hour appeared to chill the first flush of two hearts meeting.

Edgar and Judith, about 1974.

At dinner, a few nights later, I became aware that Judith knew why I was in Paris. She had been told of my physical and emotional journey. It was an unspoken frame to our growing affection. She told me of her family roots. She was the daughter of a father who reported every morning to the assembly lines of Akron's tire manufacturing plants. Every morning, every week, every year. She had been determined to abandon the prescribed order of church-defined happiness for young women from Cuyahoga Falls, Ohio—find a husband, raise the children, keep a neat house.

The United States Information Agency, with its travel poster allure of overseas assignments, was her exit. From the beginning, Judith had moved rapidly from a generic secretary to the executive assistant to the director of USIA in whatever country she was assigned.

But that first dinner date not only encouraged my already rapid heartbeat, it collided with a more threatening reality. Judith's Paris assignment was temporary to fill a short-term vacancy. Very short. She had thirty days before reporting to her permanent post in Vienna. It occurred to me that the abrupt departure of the heroine in my family's annals of romance appeared to be a multi-generational problem. I pictured Gaston Bloch, my grandfather, in pursuit of the girl next door, a chase that spanned an ocean, not to mention two continents, from Alsace to the frontier of San Antonio, Texas.

A century later his grandson could take some comfort that there was a Paris–Vienna express train to assist in proposing another option to the lady of the latest drama. My plea was less than subtle: I really miss you. Come back to Paris. Move into that Île Saint-Louis perch overlooking the Seine, "and we will live happily ever after..." The offer was accepted, possibly with some unspoken reservation about that last part. It was followed, two years later, with my more formal proposal that would bring us to that Mediterranean village in the hills of Provence.

Judith and I had adopted Mons like Pierre and Monique Carrere had adopted us as les cousins Américains. Their Mons outpost was the family summer rendezvous. Because of our acceptance in the clan and regular holiday and summer appearances, we were allowed to share a slice of village life.

When our official marriage banns were literally tacked to the front door of the village hall—an historical tradition that might have accommodated a father with serious doubts about a prospective son-in-law, or another suitor with a better offer—many in the village were surprised that our intended status was not already our status. But in the tradition of discretion in les affaires de coeur, *matters of the heart,* no one even raised an eyebrow. Judith, in fact, had established her own reputation on the village's important evaluation scale of summer visitors: success at boules.

"La belle blonde Américaine,"–*the beautiful blonde American*–"elle est bien forte"–*she's really good at pétanque.* It was no small compliment. Boules de pétanque is an uncompromising part of the holy trinity that makes a village a village in southern France. A church, the café of course, and the (relatively) flat, chestnut tree-shaded village pétanque court. It is there where men crouch, squint, stare and silently plot the trajectory of a polished steel ball in pursuit of le bouchon, the small wooden ball that is the target of the game. The competitor whose steel ball stops closest to le bouchon is the winner and, generally, the beneficiary of several aperitifs from the café, conveniently never more than a few steps away.

The presiding bishops of the pétanque court are the most dedicated, talented players. It is they who determine the order of matters. Women are rarely invited to step out from the spectator ranks.

"La belle blonde Américaine" somehow managed to earn a special exception in this male dominated terrain whose elderly members still harbored wishful memories that could be briefly restored at the sight of an attractive woman.

Like in all villages, in Mons a hierarchy determined the status of its inhabitants—both year round and those who came for les grandes vacances. The August vacation, a near sacred national ritual, brings the workaday habits of France to a celebratory summer festival halt. Generally, a month-long, halt.

At the top of the pyramid of influence are les monsois, the natives, divided into special sub-groups as the purveyors of life's necessities: the postman, the grocer, the baker and, certainly, the dispenser of wine with his regiment of bottled spirits that are served as aperitif or digestive before and after any dinner worth mentioning. In a village of 254, necessity requires some double duty. In Mons the guardianship of the fruit of the vine—or more accurately, its squeezed and fermented juices—was entrusted to Monsieur et Madame Lambert, the proprietors of the village grocery store.

Included in the higher echelons of village respect were the black-clad widows of husbands who held rank and privileges in past years. They were always addressed as Madame, sometimes even by their peers, and certainly by the younger generation. When a heavy piece of furniture had to be moved or more urgently, a bonbonne, a cask of wine, wrestled up a narrow stairway, there always were younger hands to help.

The summer visitors, too, had a pecking order. There were subtle distinctions if you came from distant Paris or from the closer coastal cities of Marseille or Nice. There may have been a slight advantage if you were French, but not assuredly. Dutch, English, Swedes and Norwegians, refugees from their dark winters, were welcomed on the cobble-stoned, narrow streets of the village.

Edgar and Judith in Switzerland, 1978.

Judith and I, les Américains, were assigned a space somewhere in between, at least until our marriage banns were posted on the village hall door. I thought there was a perceptible uptick in our status as soon as the news of our intentions spread. That progress was clearly measurable at the café where congratulatory glasses were offered in such profusion that they distorted my navigational ability no matter what time of day.

My friend, Monsieur Mirreur, the village game warden, was a significant contributor to this loss of equilibrium, long before the villagers had any inkling of our plans. Monsieur Mirreur had a face that might have been sculpted from the dual masks of comedy and tragedy. In his case, it was mostly the wide smile of comedy.

Monsieur Mirreur was unavoidable. Literally. His house was stationed like a toll booth on the main path just before the bakery. Every morning I would go for a loaf of fresh-baked bread that had just made its aromatic exit from the wood-fired oven. There was Mirreur. Sitting on his stoop with that mask of comedy firmly planted on his face.

"Bonjour Edgardo," he would shout in greeting, "la goûta." The wave of his hand left no doubt that I had been summoned. "La goûta"—*the taste*—was Provençal, a regional dialect with Latin ancestry traceable to the village's beginnings. The clear firewater known more popularly as Marc, registered an alcohol level in the upper reaches of a scale that started at a hefty 100 proof. Monsieur Mirreur made it himself, every fall, dispensing it daily throughout the year to ward off any malady you want to name, an inoculation both for himself and for friends who inevitably would pass by.

As game warden, Mirreur not only knew the most likely location of a wild hare but, more relevant, he was an authority on identifying the village widow who could best turn it into a Michelin Guide rated rabbit stew. Naturellement, the donor would be invited.

Monsieur Mirreur was among our expanding cohort in our summer village that helped us graduate from a polite bonjour for strangers when passing in the narrow byways, to three—definitely three—kisses on alternating cheeks, the habitual greeting among friends. In Mirreur's case, the greeting frequently was warmed with a glass of his homemade medication.

Our expanding roster of village friends led naturally to a growing wedding guest list, growing and growing. In the end, a good part of the village came. At the conclusion of Mayor Audibert's nerve-jangling ceremony, we marched in what can only be described as a free form column from the village hall to the Carrere summer house on the outskirts. When we passed the café, the usual habitués had assembled in front, raising their glasses: "Vive le mariage! Vive le mariage!"

With the cheers for the wedding couple, I knew that our village status had moved perceptibly from summer visitor to a new rank on the social scale of Mons.

At Muckross, in 1981.

Weddings, particularly in southern France, are celebratory pinnacles that are sensitively constructed on a foundation of toasts, joy, laughter, and, bien sûr–*of course*, the gastronomy of local delicacies. These are accompanied by a profusion of apé-ritifs, cognacs, Pastis (the local favorite), home brews like those designed by Monsieur Mirreur, and wine. Many, many bottles of wine. In our case, an entire antique tin bathtub full. To be more precise, 54 liters for fewer than 100 wedding guests.

A second reality of weddings in le Midi, the south of France, is that a clock and the specific recordings of its dials are not necessarily a ruling factor in the sequence of events. Time is a variable perception, often calibrated to the noonday sun and its temperature. Any designated hour is moveable, frequently dependent on how hot it is according to the energy level of the time keeper.

For les Américains, schooled in the Anglo-Saxon ways of promptness, this Mediterranean variable time piece required more than a dollop of controlled anxiety. As we left for the ceremony, the field next door, designated as the site for the reception, was an undisturbed scene of tranquility. Only the chirping cicadas announced their presence in a tableau that fronted dramatically on the heat-shrouded hills and valleys below.

"Pas de problème," Monsieur Lambert, the village grocer, assured us in the planning stage after he volunteered to be our caterer. He would locate the tables and chairs, checkered table-cloths, "tous"–*everything*. He would make a special voyage to the larger villages below for the delicacies that were beyond those on the shelves of his store.

"Pas de problème. Enquete-vous pas." *No problem. Don't you worry.*

Little did we know that Monsieur Lambert was an expert in evaluating the relativity of time in le Midi. He was certain, absolutely certain, that a wedding scheduled for four o'clock in the afternoon had not even a remote chance of commencing at four o'clock.

He was right. More relevant, when we arrived after the village hall ceremony, the field next door was a Renoir painting come to life. Long tables with a small vase of wild flowers on each, and a center structure of gastronomic opulence—pâtés, salads, olives green and black, pickled eggplant, cornichons, the tiny brined gherkins that invariably accompany pâté. And the cheeses, with their own separate place of honor, a cascade of such numerous varieties that they added credence to President de Gaulle's observation, "How can you govern a country that has 435 varieties of cheese?"

The desserts commanded their own territory. A separate table of apple and peach fruit tarts, layer cakes with shimmering chocolate covering, whip cream-kissed wild strawberries and miniature pastries in such profusion that a quandary of choice confronted each wedding guest.

The festivities began with an appropriate blessing, delivered by our friend, the priest from Montauroux, l'Abbé Beal. Like his counterpart in America, my friend Monsignor Geno Baroni, l'Abbé was sensitive to the religious diversity of the occasion and took care to request from God a generic, one-size-fits-all blessing for the newlyweds. There were numerous toasts, varying in length and elegance. I thought the quality and quantity might have been in direct proportion to the diminishing content in the antique bathtub.

Because the festivity was located on a curve of the road leading to the larger communities in the valley below, the wedding gained additional guests attracted by the celebration. The village mason, curious about the joyful sounds, stopped with his 91-year-old mother. They joined to raise their glass to our future and stayed for the duration. The postmaster, too, made periodic pilgrimages. He delivered telegrams that repeatedly included the opening phrase "best wishes." By the last delivery, after his personal toast to our wedding bliss had accompanied each previous stop, he had gained enough confidence—and wine—to read "best *weeshes*" aloud with yet another raised glass and a salutary wave to the assembled.

The laughter, the toasts, the lavish tables of delicacies and the babble of celebrants in the lavender-scented field are the time-honored staples of a French country summer wedding. At ours, the only Americans in sight were the two principals and Judith's best friend. It was a collection of villagers and neighbors. Monsieur Quatresous, a pétanque advisor to Judith; Madame Pelassi, a next door neighbor and recognized authority on wine-marinated lapin, the rabbit stew she sometimes prepared for us; Jeannine and Robert Lambert, the designers of the wedding feast; Madame Morrell, another neighbor, who until the wedding day, we only had seen wrapped in her ever-present wool housecoat no matter what time of day. And, of course, Monsieur Mirreur, who brought a special flask for la goûta in honor of the day.

It was Madame Morrell, dressed in her Sunday-go-to-Mass best, who attracted Judith's attention. Beyond her sudden sartorial transformation, there still was something different. Judith noticed that Madame Morrell didn't have a plate. She wasn't eating. Judith offered to get her some of the delicacies.

"Non, non. Merci," Madame Morrell said, pointing to her mouth. "Je ne peux pas manger. Mes dents..." *I can't eat. My teeth...*

Judith and Edgar, late 1980s.

Judith immediately recognized the difference. Madame Morrell, for the first time, in honor of this event, was wearing her false teeth that had been resting undisturbed, in a small box in her linen closet all the time we knew her. Madame Morrell, who had abandoned the comfort of her housecoat, resplendent in her special dress, was wearing teeth in our honor. That may have been the most meaningful gift of our affection-filled day.

The next morning after the train station farewell kisses from Pierre and Monique and our other adopted French cousins, we returned to Paris. We packed and toasted our farewells at the Île Saint-Louis café with the concierge news network, at the bakery, the cheese store, with the horse meat lady, and all the touchstones of our island life.

That night, our last in Paris, Jim and Gloria Jones took us to dinner across the river, at La Tour d'Argent, the three-star temple of gastronomy. We sat at a window table with its view of our balcony. The flower boxes, sans rocket launch pads, were in full summer bloom. The maître d' knew us as his island neighbors and offered glasses of champagne with a toast to all the joys that marriage can bring.

A wedding is life's most spectacular renewal, a flowering of optimism, a blossoming of hope for the tomorrows to come. Ours may have been a little more than that. It meant I could go home again.

Au revoir, Paris!

CHAPTER TEN

Legislature

My foray into Vermont politics started with a strategy session in my living room at Muckross in Springfield. Several friends had suggested I run for a seat in the Vermont House of Representatives.

Judith and I had been home from Paris less than a year. After the accident that simple word "home" had become an obstacle for me. A threat, a discomfort. It was another mountain to climb. I had not been inside the Vermont house since Louise and I drove out of the road for the last time. I couldn't face it. I couldn't return to all those familiar things, the small knickknacks that had meaning only for Louise and me because they illuminated a memory we shared. The objects had become haunting scars, markers of gloom. But this "home coming" with Judith was a time of renewal. A rebirth, with wondrous warmth that radiates from two shared lives.

That evening's political discussion, however, was much more earthbound. Romance was not among the living room guests. The voices were not much different than those in hundreds of embryonic meetings where a group of citizens search for a candidate to carry their banner of change. No different, at least, until I asked a conversation-stopping question: "What makes you think a Democrat can get elected here?"

Suddenly the room was silent. A near visible stillness, interrupted by a clearing of throats; sounds you hear only when there is a sudden, unexpected pause in a room filled with conversation.

"You're not going to run as a *Democrat?*"

There was a tone of incredulity in the rising pitch of the inquiry. It was a question less framed by paranoia, and more by long, very long, uninterrupted history—no Democrat ever had been elected in my legislative district. Only one had occupied a seat. And that was a temporary aberration when the Republican incumbent had unexpectedly died. Philip Hoff, the first Democratic Governor of Vermont in 109 years, appointed Ben Bloomfield, a Democrat, to complete the departed's term. In the next election voters reverted to their century-old habit. They elected his Republican opponent even though Springfield was a blue collar union town that most likely would have voted Democratic if the town had been located anywhere but in solid Republican Vermont.

The steep political hill climb was best illustrated a little more than a decade earlier when John F. Kennedy lost the town by better than 2 to 1. Democrats were a curiosity, an oddity, like a Vermont Christmas without snow. They were infrequently sighted and even less often self-confessed, at least in public. They were seen only in significant flocks in an urban political oasis like Burlington and a few locations that barely met the definition of cities in the most rural state in the nation. In the legislature they were a predictable, consistent minority whose underdog status traced its lonely lineage to the party's beginning. Elections in Vermont were decided in the primary, where Republicans would compete against their brethren to get their party's nomination. That was the end of it. No one needed to stay up late to find out who won in November.

Governor Thomas Salmon used to relish telling the election night story—only slightly embellished—about counting votes in a small Vermont town. "Republican, Republican, Republican, Republican, Democrat. Ah, looks like Shaunessy voted," the tabulator pronounced before continuing. "Republican, Republican, Republican, Democrat. Can you believe it! That Shaunessy voted twice!"

It is these artifacts of history and folklore that put a pall over that meeting in our living room. It was sufficiently dark and somber that my friends convinced me that we needed to form another political party, adding an Independent Party line on the ballot for the orthodox who were convinced their fingers would shrivel if they ever put an X after a Democrat's name. It was a precautionary strategy, born out of bitter memories of Vermont suffering higher casualties than any other state on the bloody battlefields of the Civil War.

But the memories were blunted by two key factors. First, a quantum change in Vermont's demographics, pushed by increasing migrations of urban refugees to a state that offered a chance to grow your own vegetables in home gardens, to wear sweaters and parkas to mark the change of seasons, to sniff the fall-tinged wood smoke, and, most important, a chance to abandon big city anonymity. At the local general store they actually called you by your name whenever you came in, even if you just bought the local weekly paper. You were a real person. You had a name of your own. That helped shape a new politics. The newcomers were not fused to the revered hereditary Republican dynasty.

The second shift in the political terrain is summarized by the dictum of former U.S. House of Representative Speaker "Tip" O'Neill: "All politics is local." A few of us distilled that even further. Politics, in this micro environment, meant voters could get a look at you, listen to your ideas, size you up. This political art form, fashioned by the perennial underdogs, was called "going door to door." Its practitioners obscured their political labels because they became flesh and blood people, a neighbor standing in the doorway of another who shared a community both called home. The party label became less important. In my first modest political brochure the word "Democrat" could not be found. It simply said: "If you vote for the man..."

It was a stealth campaign. The Republicans still were warmed by roughly 200 years of election outcomes, a history that had become a political narcotic, dulling the senses of change around them.

Judith and I started the vote quest in late spring, focusing on the street map of our district. One neighborhood, one street at a time. Years later I thought campaigning was as exhilarating, sometimes more so, than actually serving. I learned about my neighbors, their children and their school progress or lack of it, about an occasional relative with problems. Night after night, I was educated about what really mattered to them. It trumped any sociology class I had ever taken.

Every weekday evening we would start at about 4 p.m. The starting time was no accident. In a town with generally both parents working, any earlier effort was greeted only by a barking dog. Judith, a natural, gentle touch campaigner, would take one side of a street, and I would take the other. At each door she would offer to bring me over if they had questions.

Swearing in a new voter.

In the first week we learned several lessons. First, how many people were pleased that we showed up. And how many were not registered to vote. I became a notary public, my license to register voters on the spot. The most persuasive lesson, though, was a more immediate threat: dogs. We were startled by how many were in our district. More relevant, that almost all of them had a negative attitude about door knocking strangers, particularly aspiring politicians.

Solving the canine threat became a campaign necessity. Before we left for our appointed rounds we made a special check that we had campaign brochures, voter registration forms and the bag of bribery biscuits. Their potential for canine silence was confirmed several times on just about every street. A very few times, when greeted by a German Shepherd or a pit bull, we saw no need to test our bribe-to-silence theory. We skipped that stop.

After every house call we would review each conversation and rate it—a "Yes," a "Maybe," or a flat out "No Way." Each positive and each hopeful was recorded in a running log book for future follow up. Sometimes, however, my exuberance for campaigning ran substantially ahead of my political pragmatism.

One of those moments began on the porch of Stella Walsh's farm house on a rural country road that paralleled the Connecticut River. Stella was in the kitchen, screen door ajar, listening to the Red Sox while canning tomatoes. At 92, she was a popular fixture in the district because she was the oldest living graduate of our high school, a distinction that earned her a chauffeured open convertible at the front of the annual alumni parade. A banner on the car announced her status.

She listened patiently as I explained the essence of our visit.

"What partee are you runnin' undah?"

"I'm a Democrat."

The sound of the radio announcer bemoaning a Red Sox strikeout filled the void. Her facial expression I thought had suddenly taken on a few extra wrinkles. "Ohhh... I'm sorry... " she said. "I've voted Republican ever since I could."

Whether it was the sunny early fall afternoon or the portrait of a 92-year-old canning tomatoes and cheering on her Red Sox, the scene carried me into the shimmering warmth of Americana celebrated, sometimes uniquely, on a *Saturday Evening Post* cover. I offered her a ride to the polls on Election Day.

We were hardly out of earshot when Judith stared at me. "You just offered to drive that lady to the polls who just told you she isn't going to vote for you?"

I had no answer except a sheepish nod of guilt.

That first summer of door-to-door campaigning turned out to be more than a political strategy. It was an affirmation of why we had come home. It filled a blank space in our lives—that void was the absence of a sense of community. We understood that we needed to belong to a group that shared some common goals and some common fears. For me, it meant roots in the soil of permanence, a place I could call home again.

In France I was a spectator—a clinical, unattached observer of the public issues of our days, whether the drama was in France or in America. I was in spatial orbit where my two planets were visible, but too distant to recruit me into the army of protest or change. Most every morning I would read the *International Herald Tribune* and *Le Figaro*, the French daily. At the end of this morning ritual I was insulated from the latest crisis at home because it was too far away, and yesterday's turmoil—or most likely, strike—in France... well, it was really not my country. I was just a spectator, emotionally shielded from either guilt or shame.

It was not only a sense of community that grew out of that summer of campaigning. It was a clear understanding how one individual, if part of a majority in a 150 member legislature, might influence some of the most basic parts of daily life. It is our state governments that set the moral guide posts of our communities. Often they determine family well-being, partially dependent on a mandated minimum wage, or an effort to abolish or reaffirm the death penalty, whether we execute the most violent among us or incarcerate them for life; or maybe the decisions that impact the very personal right of a woman to make a choice about having an unwanted child.

A door-to-door campaign propels these public issues from academic theory and clinical case studies into the pragmatic challenge of raising a family. I learned the essentials about the minimum wage in a kitchen in a public housing complex in my district. My instructors were a couple with four children. He was a mechanic and she worked as a chambermaid at a nearby tourist resort. The gallon of milk and its companion loaf of bread on the kitchen table were mute testimony that it took an hour of minimum wage labor—making beds and cleaning toilets—to buy them.

That fall, I won in a landslide with 50% more votes than the nearest candidate. The margin was a surprise to everyone, including to Judith and me.

The door-to-door personal effort became a campaign staple even in the years when I ran for the Senate where my district was so huge that we could meet only a tiny fraction of its voters. They honored me with their confidence in 16 primary and general election victories. In each, except in my freshman term, I was privileged to chair a legislative committee, Health & Welfare in the House and the Appropriations Committee in the Senate.

As George Washington, with Judith in a town parade.

The truth, however, was that I was a late bloomer among political aspirants in my family. It started in the early days of the 19th century. Grandfather Gaston Bloch, after several decades as a Zurich burger, ran for the City Council, setting a benchmark his grandchildren worked hard to avoid: he lost.

But that stubborn political gene—to reject things as they are—had surfaced even earlier. It showed up in Texas where my grandfather's in-laws had immigrated in the 1880; his niece, Jennie Brunschwig, not only matched the frontier enthusiasm, but revolted against the very narrow boundaries confining women. Jennie more often was called Jimmie, a nickname that was not an accidental bow to masculine-dominated society. She was the advance "man" for what years later was called "women's liberation," even before the movement had a name.

She left little doubt about her independent ways, ignoring the male-dominated order that was venerated in and out of Texas. She cut her hair shorter than the contemporary fashion because it was easier to manage; raised her skirt hemlines higher than the modest limits prescribed for frontier ladies, and just to emphasize the point, occasionally wore pants—men's pants because stores simply didn't stock those items for women.

She received attention not only for her independence, but also for her leadership in San Antonio community organizations. With focused energy, she sold a record amount of World War I bonds. It didn't hurt either that she was an ardent, publicly recognized Democrat, one of a minority of women who attended the 1932 Democratic National convention. She was appointed postmaster, the first woman in that job. She regularly signed documents E.R. Brunschwig, judiciously camouflaging that the postmaster of Laredo actually was a post*mistress*. And, in an act of Texas-size patriotism she picked names for her children to spell LAREDO—Lionel, Andre and Raymond—running out of children before running out of letters in Laredo. The next generation tried to fix the shortfall. My cousin, Dorace, was named to fill in the missing "D."

In the current political family, my sister Madeleine had the lead role. She had established a toehold in the Vermont Legislature two years earlier, after a campaign to locate a flashing signal at a railroad crossing. She was concerned because her children had to cross those tracks on their way to school. Madeleine rose rapidly in the hierarchy of legislative influence becoming simultaneously the first woman and first Democrat to chair the House Appropriations Committee.

With my arrival, a brother and sister combination would become a curiosity, but barely a footnote in legislative history. The siblings (and occasional their sibling rivalry) produced some chortles during a few roll call votes.

"Kunin of Burlington?" the House Clerk would intone as he called, in alphabetical order, the roll of representatives on an important legislative initiative.

"Yes."

"May of Springfield?"

"No."

A murmur of snickers rustled through the ornate House Chamber as we canceled each other's vote. If the family coalition fractured it was not because of major policy differences, but because the interests of more urban Burlington occasionally were not those of my more rural southern Vermont district.

Just how rural I learned from a tiny town tacked on to my Springfield district. The town of Baltimore had all of 74 families tucked along its 7.2 miles of mostly tree-shaded dirt roads. Not a single foot was paved. It's those dirt roads that created—literally—the Town of Baltimore on October 19, 1793. But it was not until 31 years later that Baltimore got its own legislator. Benjamin Page, who Annie Pollard's history of Baltimore shows, had bought the "Jonathan Burnam place" and begun his political pilgrimage by being elected lister and highway surveyor in 1798. He became the first lawmaker from Baltimore when 28 of his neighbors—all of those qualified to vote—sent him as their man to the capitol. The move was more than a signal of local pride. It was a marriage of Vermont pragmatism wedded to the certainty of New England weather.

Every spring, more precisely, on Town Meeting Day in March, each Vermonter helps decide the year's priorities for their community. But you have to *get* there to decide. In those days, often more than half of the residents of Baltimore-to-be were blocked from attending their Town Meeting in what then was their Town of Cavendish. They had to go around Hawks Mountain, a massive barrier that separated them from the more populated area north of the peak. It was a scenic buggy or sleigh ride, depending on the season. Except, during Vermont's "fifth" season: mud season.

Teams of horses would rebel and wagons got stuck in the spring thawed quagmire. It was an annual certainty, eventually recognized as inevitable, even by the Vermont Legislature which gave a separate town charter to Baltimore so that its citizens could get to their own town meeting in their one public building, the one-room schoolhouse.

Now "mud season" is a baffling concept to the uninitiated. If you've never been mired in up-to-the-axle mud, you just don't appreciate it. In tiny Baltimore, like in other Vermont towns with dirt roads, dramatic tales of stuck-in-the-mud dramas abound. A particular folklore favorite of this annual paralysis centered on Abner and Homer.

Homer, according to generations of raconteurs, was sitting on his front porch surveying the sea of ooze in front of him when he saw a hat bobbing on its surface. He fetched a long pole and tipped up the hat to reveal his neighbor.

"Gawd Abner," he said, "you're really in it!"

"I'm alright, Homer," Abner said. "But the team is in kinda deep."

Baltimore, and its 74 families, became my favorite constituency in 16 years in the legislature. In my freshman effort, the community taught me an important lesson: I had to earn my keep. On Election Day that first year, I had fewer votes than the opposition. I started my voyage toward redemption the next spring, at Town Meeting.

A Vermont Town Meeting is not just another political gabfest. It is the purest microcosm of Democracy. Every voter becomes a legislator on the first Tuesday after the first Monday in March. A majority will decide how much money they will spend on educating their children, grading and plowing their roads, and electing their neighbors to supervise these matters. Around noon, generally, they would pause for an hour long recess so everybody could enjoy a community dinner. Most families brought a home cooked effort. I always thought that the early settlers had more than gastronomy in mind. Yankee politeness required a few admiring words about the quality of a creamy casserole or the delicacy of the buttery crusted apple pie. Never mind that 20 minutes earlier, the complimentor and its recipient were in a decibel rising dispute about repairing the old road grader or buying a new one.

It was to these Town Meetings that I was invited to give a report on the activities of the legislature and answer any question about "the doings" in the state capitol. It was a two-way communication with an imbalance in my favor. I learned more from them than they learned from me.

One year, in particular, stands out. Among the decisions required at Town Meeting was to approve their School Board-recommended education budget. The total was directly related to the amount of property tax each voter would pay next year. The bulk of these education dollars supported the red schoolhouse and its one teacher. She taught all six grades in that one large room festooned with posters, student art drawings, and a few green plants to cushion the effects of the seemingly ever-present snow drifts beyond its walls. The School Board's chairperson explained that this year the Board wanted the Town Meeting to consider making a significant change. It would cost more money—raise taxes—but provide a much better and richer education for the four sixth graders if they would be sent to the much larger junior high school in Springfield.

A small minority of voters at the meeting had school age children. The largest group was the silver-haired constituency whose children had graduated from that schoolhouse many years ago. They would pay the largest share of the extra dollars. An animated discussion followed before blank slips of paper were distributed for a "Yes" or "No" paper ballot.

The Town Moderator, a blend of referee and Town Meeting leader, announced the results.

"The Ayes have it. We're gonna send 'em."

If the town of Baltimore would have been large enough to need a mayor, the hands down choice would have been a farm wife named Margaret Hammond. She was straight talking, a bit wrinkled, a grandmotherly, apron-protected Vermonter. Even if she'd wanted to—and she surely didn't—she couldn't have wrapped any important opinion in the gauze of euphemism, even when more than a few votes were at stake.

"I can't support you," she said.

It was about her first sentence after I finished detailing why I—as a very optimistic Democrat—was running for a time honored Republican seat she once occupied. She was 74 at the time. She had just clambered down a ladder from the roof after inspecting her chimney to decide if she needed to replace a few loose bricks, or repoint them.

Margaret Hammond had been in the legislature at a time when each of the 246 towns and cities in Vermont had their own representative. It was such a dramatic political tilt that Baltimore's 134 citizens had exactly the same political power as Burlington with its 35,000 residents. Each community had one vote. The imbalance ended when Vermont was forced to reapportion by a US Supreme Court decision that told the towns they had to divvy up their legislators based on population and not on geography.

That didn't stop Margaret Hammond. She announced that she was going to run for the Vermont Senate, not only from one of the smallest towns in Vermont, but from a home base that included all of 54 registered voters, the tiniest constituency among the 14 towns that made up her senatorial district. The district was the largest in the state with more geography than some of the nation's congressional districts. She promptly won in the only election tally that counted: the Republican primary.

With that 1966 victory, Margaret Hammond became only the third woman ever elected to the Vermont Senate. She was admired not only for the Vermont virtue of brevity of speech but that it never was burdened with excess verbiage to diplomatically soften her point of view. Baltimore became known as the place where Senator Hammond came from, a place so small that it had no post office of its own, no general store or gas station. Its one public building was the one that really mattered—the one-room schoolhouse.

On that early fall afternoon of our first political discussion, after her four word pronouncement of non-support for my candidacy, she invited me into her parlor for a glass of home-made dandelion wine. The parlor, with its solid oak table and straight back chairs, was the informal office of "Baltimore Town Affairs." Not only was it the headquarters of the former Senator cum Delinquent Tax Collector, but it also was the home of her daughter, Frances Hunter, Baltimore's Town Clerk. If you needed to file a deed or wanted a fishing or hunting license, that's where you got it. The hour of your arrival didn't seem to matter. If you needed an old deed, well, that required a trip outdoors. Some of the older town records were stored in a two-ton town safe. The steel hulk was judged to be a threat to the parlor floor joists, so it was sheltered on the terra firma of the old Hammond milk house, between the barn and the house.

Rep. May at his home in Springfield.

She asked me to take a visitor's chair while she rummaged through an old file cabinet. Out came yellowed clippings that told of her efforts in the state capitol, some notes of speeches she gave, some rubber band encircled legislative journals, and few recyclable gift wrapping ribbons that had strayed into the "Political" drawer.

These mementos of the past helped illustrate the hour-long lecture of what she would do if—just supposin'—if she were in my place wanting to win a seat in the Vermont House of Representatives. She refilled my dandelion wine glass while she continued the hour-long political seminar. The word "Democrat" never was uttered by either student or professor.

A few years later, Margaret would sit, on Election Day, inside the entrance of that schoolhouse, anchored to a spot that could not be circumvented by any voter without a greeting for the retired senator. She always was a candidate for local office; most often, Baltimore's Delinquent Tax Collector. Her neighbors thought that if anybody could get a few dollars out of folks who were behind on their taxes, it would be Margaret Hammond. Her gate keeper perch clearly violated basic Vermont Election Law. It might have been an issue in bigger places, but it didn't bother the voters of Baltimore, Vermont. The law said no candidate—even an incumbent Delinquent Tax Collector—or any political campaigning can take place inside a polling place.

"Now I don't want to tell you how to vote," Margaret would announce to each arriving voter. "But that Edgar May has done a good job for Baltimore."

Several years later, when I started my Vermont Senate campaign, the natural launching pad was this smallest town of the sprawling political jurisdiction of Windsor County. It was in front of that one-room schoolhouse that I said I wanted to follow Margaret Hammond's political journey.

It was one of those Vermont days that looked like it was ripped out of a New England calendar. A half moon of maple trees ringed the red schoolhouse. Their spring greening formed a canopy, with sun and shade designs patterned on the leaves. In the pasture across the road John Thomas's herd of Guernseys, Jerseys, and Ayrshires formed a second tier of spectators—divided only by a wire fence—when their curiosity was piqued by the cars and pickups along the side of the schoolhouse road.

Margaret and Frances Hunter had organized a team of ladies who baked the cookies, the apple pies, and who brought the home-canned pickled snacks that spoke more of a summer picnic than a political meeting. Maybe it was part nostalgia, a backward leap to when life was simpler, understanding both its harshness and its softness.

It was reminiscent of the Vermont when if you got sick the neighbors will bring food and do the milking... where if you are stuck in a snow drift they always have a tractor and a chain to pull you out. The Vermont where everybody calls each other by their first names and the place you call home is still the Dixon place, never mind that Mr. Dixon had been prayerfully lowered into the stony soil of Baltimore more than a century ago.

That November when the ballot box was opened, the vote count showed that the Delinquent Tax Collector and the Senate candidate had the identical number of votes. Both Margaret and I received all but four of the total votes cast.

"He makes things happen"

The Valley News

Re-elect
Senator Edgar May

Some weeks later we discussed this conundrum. Maybe we should try and figure out who the four were who we obviously did not convince to put an X next to our name. "Maybe," Margaret's analytical bent surfaced, "maybe there might have been eight different people, four who didn't vote for you and four others who didn't vote for me." That possible accounting ended the inquiry. We decided to drop the entire matter.

Through the years, Senator Margaret Hammond kept her parlor and its memory files in order. Both were open to anyone who might stop by. She made a little dandelion wine each year until her eighty-seventh.

The day after she died, the Hammond family asked me to give the eulogy at her funeral. The Baptist Church, the family's spiritual home, was packed with a standing room overflow. For me, standing at the altar, it may have been the most honored speaking part I ever received.

CHAPTER ELEVEN

Legislature 2

The telephone on the bedside table rang incessantly. Only the pale yellow orbit circling the dials of the alarm clock pierced the darkness. They said it was 2:40 a.m. *Two–forty in the morning!* I was in that blurry no-man's land of the semi-conscious. Was it a real phone ringing or was it a repetitive jangling in my dream?

"Yes?" I croaked into the receiver.

"I know this is a bad time to call," the voice said. "But I got a helluva problem. I thought you might be the one who could help me." There was sufficient anxiety in the voice that I thought it might be bad form to remind him of the hour. "My wife went into labor about an hour ago and I called her doctor. The answering machine says he's on vacation; I should call his stand-in across the river in New Hampshire. That fella tells me to bring her over to the hospital over *there*."

Could I call the doctor, explain the situation, and convince him to make the 15 minute drive to the hospital on the Vermont side of the Connecticut River? The "situation" was summarized in two simple sentences:

"My people been Vermonters since I don't know when. I can't have my kid have to say that he was born in New Hampshire."

Calling yourself a native Vermonter—"born right here in town"—has a pedigree of its own. It is a special status that differentiates you from those who came from "A-way." Some of us were about 200 years tardy, after Ethan Allen laid claim to the peaks and valleys of the Green Mountains. The latecomers were baptized "Flatlanders." Fortunately, for me, I was able to mute this deficiency a bit. "Wasn't born here," I would confess and then immediately launch into a salvage operation, "But it's very hard to call somebody born in Switzerland a flatlander."

It was not an accident of history that Vermont was the 14th State to enter the Union. After the Revolution, it rejected joining the 13 original colonies. Instead its citizens declared themselves an independent nation—a smidgen of a Republic that was a sliver between the embryonic United States and Canada. They held out until 1791.

In what would become a habit of plowing new ground, Vermont's constitution was the first to outlaw slavery. The trend setting continued. On a per capita basis, Vermont had the highest enlistment rate of any state in both the Civil War's Union Army and in the early days of the Peace Corps. Just for good measure, in 1940 its legislature declared war on Germany months before the United States. Going down a different (often snow covered) road became a Vermont virtue, a folk tale of independence. It's been nurtured ever since.

In any litany of self-proclaimed superiority, however, there is the temptation to expunge the shared human frailties that fester no matter what place you might call home. Vermonters, with their independence (some called it stubbornness), were and are not immune. Edna L. Beard is celebrated as the first woman elected to the Vermont House of Representatives from the tiny town of Orange, a scant 16 months after women got the right to vote. She won her seat when each town, no matter how small, had its own representative in the legislature. She won with a total of 119 votes, topping her male opponent, B. L. Richardson, who got 81.

Less frequently recalled in the warmth of memory is the reception she received in 1921 on the first day of the legislature. That's when seats are assigned. In a bow to male chivalry, Speaker of the House Franklin S. Billings, Sr. gave Representative Beard first choice of a seat in the ornate House chamber. She picked an inconspicuous No.146 in the 246 seat chamber. As the names of the other members were called, the seats beside her remained empty. When finally someone agreed to sit next to Edna Beard, the choice was greeted by catcalls and laughter.

Alexander Twilight, a black man, was elected to the Vermont legislature nearly 30 years before President Abraham Lincoln signed the Emancipation Proclamation. More than a century later, Vermont was not insulated against the civil rights storm that raged beyond its borders. In Irasburg, a small community that had a minister who happened to be black and, in 1968, was hounded out of town after a drive-by shooting and a rumor he was having an affair with a white woman.

What clearly is different, though, is that Vermont, a state with its 621,760 souls (about the population of the city of Boston), is more a state of mind than a state. That's not just quaint self-esteem. Marketing studies show that when a "Made in Vermont" label is on the package, sales increase 15%.

It's a place where people call their political folk by their first names because they see them at the local store and in the stands at the Saturday afternoon high school football game. In later years, when someone called me "Senator May" it made me uneasy. I feared the formality signaled that I was in trouble.

Among the first most important campaign advice I received was: "*Never, never* say anything really bad about your opponent. You just might be talking to his second cousin once removed or, worse yet, to his mother."

These personal relationships temper the more caustic political rhetoric. Furthermore, no matter how far politically apart adversaries might be, they share a unifying and common challenge: winter. Its frozen reality of up-to-the-eaves snow drifts and ice storm-glazed roads construct a sense of communal immobility. This periodic, forced togetherness creates community whether you like it or not. Daytime disputes in a legislative chamber are shelved in favor of the nightly card games and shared suppers, often spiced with political gossip. There is no political party litmus test for joining either tribal habit.

Vermont has a citizen legislature where regular work-a-day routines of its members are suspended in the winter months so citizen lawmakers can adjust, amend or change the way they and their neighbors govern themselves. It is Civics 101, a graying, sometimes a little boring textbook of democracy. A little boring until you realize that you're the one helping to write the latest edition. Both the burden and the exhilaration of this special authorship exploded on me in the first few months of my freshman legislative year. I had been appointed to the Judiciary Committee.

It was a gray, getting-ready-to-snow day. The small committee room was stuffy, packed with the press, television cameras and the few spectators who could squeeze into the available space. The proposal: should Vermont abolish the death penalty?

Like abortion, the question was marinated more in emotion than in fact. A newspaper poll made it clear that a majority of our fellow citizens didn't want to dismantle the electric chair. I looked around the room at my colleagues. A couple of housewives, a plumber, an insurance salesman, a couple of lawyers. Eleven of us—surrogates for all Vermonters—would decide if the worst among us would live or die. Because of the Judiciary Committee's reputation for doing its homework, a strong committee vote most likely would be validated by the full House of Representatives.

It was a particularly meaningful moment for me. Decades earlier, as a young reporter I had covered the capture of the last two men to be executed for murder in Vermont. I had interviewed Donald Demag and Francis Blair before they were dispatched to death row. They were flesh and blood people, visible in my mind's eye, each with his personal story of failure. Since their execution, the authority of the state to take a life of one who took a life continued on the books, but no judge had sentenced a murderer to die. This vote formally and legally could eliminate any death sentence in Vermont.

The chairman asked the clerk to call the roll. The room suddenly was silent, a black, midnight stillness. Only the barely perceptible whirr of the television cameras and a reporter's stifled cough were heard. The committee clerk called the members' names, punctuating each with an unemotional vocal question mark.

"May?" the clerk asked.

"Yes."

Eleven of us voted, 8 to 3, to eliminate state-sponsored executions in Vermont. Days later the full House of Representatives followed our lead, but the Senate rejected the proposal. It took another five years before both legislative chambers agreed to abolish the death penalty.

Public policy making in Vermont is shaped by more than our micro-society and that we call each other by our first names. It often sprouts from personal experience and not from a phalanx of lobbyists who propel self-interest issues onto the screen of public awareness. You're told about problems by a neighbor who comes to visit. They are talked about at the local gas station when you fill up, or when you are having coffee at the down street café.

Vermont's strict environmental laws—pushed by a Republican governor elected in part because of his reputation as a business leader—made national news not because of scientific studies presented in a white-walled legislative committee room. Governor Deane Davis became an environmental advocate after he saw raw sewage running down a southern Vermont mountainside in the wake of helter-skelter ski chalet construction. It was personal, right there in front of him. He could see it and, depending on which way the wind was blowing that day, smell it.

It is because of a personal experience like the governor's that I introduced legislation that created an Independence Fund. The legislation called for expanded in-home services to the elderly so they could stay in their own homes.

The proposal began its journey into Vermont law not because of a stack of studies about the perils of aging, but because in my door-to-door campaigning I visited several nursing homes in my district. It was in these geriatric warehouses that I saw and smelled the disinfectant sprayed rooms for our frail elderly, sitting in wheelchairs, often in silent clusters, a few staring intently at a curtained window. I was convinced there had to be a better way.

A citizen legislature is more than a sum of its diverse parts. It becomes the pathway that transports real, sometimes highly emotional problems into the forum where they just may find a solution. It is the place where its members construct the moral compass for the mini-societies within their borders. Fundamental personal freedoms are enumerated and enshrined in Vermont's appropriately colored green law books. They define right from wrong, spanning the profound to the trivial. Whether to execute a multiple killer or affirm the right to buy a can of beer on the morning of the Lord's Day, a time our forbearers ordained that all law-abiding citizens should be in church, repenting for the already accumulated sins of the week.

Among the profound and most intense emotional debates was *abortion*. The right of a woman to terminate a pregnancy. It is a legislative trigger word that instantly gets everybody to choose sides. All the medical studies and a phalanx of expert witnesses don't change anything. You're either in favor, or you're not.

The issue had been dormant for several years until a bill appeared in my Health and Welfare committee that called for outlawing all abortions in Vermont except in a few rare circumstances. I knew the vote in my committee before the first witness appeared. The proposed abortion ban would be defeated by a substantial majority. Knowing the outcome, however, was no assurance of a calm legislative voyage for such an emotionally singed issue. Both sides—Right to Life and Planned Parenthood—wanted a klieg-lighted stage to illuminate their version of the drama: To hold a public hearing in the biggest room in the State House, and inform the press, print, radio and, above all, television. We'll give you a list of our witnesses.

I refused. Not only because both sides knew as well as I did the outcome of a final committee vote, but because an emotion-fueled spectacle would only lacerate deeply held religious beliefs, without changing the final tally. I was particularly concerned about one committee member, Rep. Mary Evelti of Burlington. In any Hollywood film she would have been cast as a grandmotherly lawmaker, most likely playing opposite

Gary Cooper or Jimmy Stewart. She was a devout Catholic who was widowed at a young age and raised nine children by herself.

I explained to her there would be no circus-like public hearing. The debate would be confined to our committee room with three witnesses, each provided one-half hour to make their case: the Vermont Commissioner of Health, a spokesperson for Planned Parenthood, and a spokesperson for Right to Life. Each group would choose their own witness.

In the periodic high drama episodes of our legislature, I would sometimes think of the perfect response to a specially heated moment, unfortunately long after the debate ended, often at midnight, during the multiple mental replays of the day's drama. This time, it was different. The witness for the Right to Life movement was a physician, Dr. Felix Callahan, a tall, articulate doctor who didn't need a stethoscope around his neck to signal his medical authority. He brought a large paper bag to the witness table and started to reach for the outsize jar it contained. The television cameras and I immediately focused on the content of the jar as it was barely out of the bag. It was a near fully formed fetus floating in a formaldehyde solution.

"Dr. Callahan," I said. "There will be no such exhibits in this committee."

The glass jar was midway in its journey to the witness table. Dr. Callahan's arm paused like it was the center piece of a frozen frame in a home movie projector. There was a sudden stillness in the packed committee room.

"Dr. Callahan, there will be no such exhibits in this committee room," I repeated.

That evening the television news programs showed the entire drama, including a full explanation of the intended exhibit. The effort to outlaw abortion ended that night in the televised demonstration of excess zealotry.

Senator May in his office at Muckross.

Sometimes, in a mini-society like Vermont, a public policy shift has its birth place a continent away. A motor vehicle law change began its gestation cycle in Paris, at the residence of the American Ambassador to France.

It was one of those large receptions at the Ambassador's home, a potpourri of diversity that Ambassador Sarge Shriver loved to construct. It included political luminaries, a sprinkling of Davis Cup tennis players, a few French literary stars plucked from the pages of *Paris Match*, and a squadron of higher echelon Foreign Service officers who are expertly schooled in this social diplomacy.

I happened to be in the courtyard when a polished Rolls Royce drove through the gates. Madame Ambassadress Eunice Kennedy Shriver had invited her sister-in-law, Jackie Kennedy Onassis and her husband, Ari, to the reception.

I knew Jackie from previous meetings and welcomed them as they stepped out of the Rolls. It was when I escorted them to the entrance that I was startled by a flash of home on the front of the limousine. A shiny, green Vermont license plate.

Years later that Paris courtyard scene reappeared. The Commissioner of Motor Vehicles was testifying about his annual budget before the Senate Appropriations Committee. I recounted the Paris scene and asked, "Commissioner, why would a Rolls Royce in Paris have a Vermont license plate?"

The Commissioner smiled. "Mr. Chairman," he said, "probably because we have a $15,000 limit on how much we tax luxury cars. If they register a car in Vermont worth a lot more, they pay sales tax on only the first $15,000."

After the hearing I asked a staff member to research the number of luxury cars licensed in Vermont. It was a surprising list. There were Lamborghinis, Ferraris, Mercedes, Rolls— probably many of them had never traversed a mile of Vermont highway. The tax limit meant that Vermont drivers were subsidizing the transportation of the affluent because insurance rates were, in part, based on annual repair costs. Much higher luxury car repair costs around the world drove rising Vermont insurance rates.

A few days later the Appropriations Committee voted unanimously to eliminate the tax ceiling.

Sometimes significant public policy hinges on an incidental, but very rural problem. One of those featured a herd of

202 | EDGAR MAY

cows whose path to their barn was cut off by a brand new interstate highway. A cow tunnel became the improbable catalyst that changed a vote to construct a new juvenile jail.

The Senate Appropriations Committee had voted to deny the governor a separate and larger juvenile jail by a narrow 4 to 3 vote. The majority believed a larger jail would be filled by young people who could be better served in less stringent community facilities. Between the first and second required confirming vote, a Senator from dairy farm-populated Franklin County changed his mind. He had met with the governor (who happened to be my relative) and left the discussion with what I believed was a promise of a cow tunnel for a farmer in his district. The chairman of the Appropriations Committee had no cow tunnels in his kitbag of legislative baubles. The jail was built.

Occasionally, however, trying to solve a local problem falls squarely into the terrain of unintended consequences. Remember that 2:40 a.m. phone call about the perils of having a Vermont-conceived baby born in New Hampshire? The call prompted what I thought was a very modest change in the law. My bill simply proposed that if a Vermont mother gave birth in a neighboring state because Vermont medical care was not available, the local town clerk could issue a Vermont birth certificate for the new arrival.

Well! All hell broke loose. The furies were ignited by federal officials who spend their government lives counting every one of the roughly 300 million of us. Not just enumerating each of us, but placing us, for posterity, in the state of our arrival. The United States Census Bureau erupted in high statistical dudgeon. Census Bureau press releases rolled off the mimeograph machines. Calls to the Vermont congressional delegation followed.

"How can we officially report a birth in Vermont when, actually, the baby first arrived in New Hampshire?" A conundrum that neither my agitated, past-midnight caller or his legislative helper could answer. The bill died a quiet death.

The task of "modifying" a coveted Vermont native label, however, was not a passing legislative distraction. It continued to smolder and surfaced again in the first decade of the new century. Nearly 25 years later the handicap's lead actor was a Dr. William Bloom, a prominent neurosurgeon, whose planned birthplace was pre-empted by an insurmountable Vermont barrier: a blizzard. Both the House and the Senate offered a modest remedy. They voted to designate Dr. Bloom "an honorary native Vermonter." The Joint Resolution said:

> Whereas, individuals who were born in the Green Mountain State are rightfully proud of their social status as native Vermonters, and, Whereas, while a flatlander may reside in Vermont nearly an entire lifetime, and make an indelible contribution to the quality of life in this State, a flatlander still has not earned the right to be called a native Vermonter, and Whereas, although Dr. William Bloom did not actually enter this world within the geographic confines of Vermont, having been born at his parents' home in Granville, N.Y., he was, however, conceived in Poultney and, had it not been for a blizzard, would have been born at the Rutland [Vt.] hospital...

Joint Resolution 6 passed unanimously without a peep from the United States Census Bureau.

The House of Representatives in my years as a member was a homey, laid back place. Every morning started with a clergyman appealing for guidance from a higher authority and a bowed-head request to bless our deliberations. This was followed by giving lawmakers the chance to introduce their visiting guests seated in the gallery. These might have included the sixth grade class from Pomfret Elementary School on a "Civics Day" outing, the local fire chief (an influential ally on Election Day) who would testify that morning before a legislative committee, and a cousin who may have had the handicap of calling home a place from "A-way." Each introduction was followed by customary lawmakers' applause, cementing the special moment into a galaxy where each guest, for an in-the-spotlight moment, was a star.

The House of Representatives was a place where an emotion-fringed, sonorous speech, punctuated by arm waving emphasis, could carry along a dozen "undecideds" who sometimes wait for guidance from some of their respected brethren. In the Senate such a William Jennings Bryan oratorical moment may, just occasionally, earn a faint, appreciative nod from another senator, but it rarely shifts his vote. When a majority vote needs just 16 senators, you best do your persuading and vote counting in the hallways before the first drop of the morning gavel.

After my apprentice first term in the "People's House" I was named Chairman of the House Committee on Health and Welfare. Among its newly appointed members was a freshman legislator who would leave a colorful and a finely honed political edge on this citizen legislature. This particular citizen was the member from Bennington, Ralph Wright.

It was evident that his sojourn in my committee was only a way station, a political basic training for his future role as Speaker of the House of Representatives. His political molding was less traceable to the genteel atmosphere of Bennington College, his home district intellectual emporium, than to the pragmatic neighborhood curriculum of his native South Boston. A major in "Street Smarts," and a minor in "Sharp Elbows" were essential requirements for graduation. It was apparent after the first week in my committee that the member from Bennington's role model was more likely the loquacious Tip O'Neill of Massachusetts rather than the taciturn Calvin Coolidge of Vermont.

When not in the legislature, Representative Wright was a school teacher, leading an alternative educational program for the toughest kids in the school district. I always thought it was a match that must have been designed beyond the stratosphere of mere mortals. Ralph's rapport with his charges was a near symbiotic marriage. The teacher and the student understood each other, sometimes cloned by their distinctive high wire performances without benefit of a net.

No Ralph Wright escapade illustrated this better than on the opening day of his second term. The political terrain had shifted to a new Republican Speaker, who according to custom, named the most neophyte and newest arrivals to the dreary task of counting and certifying the election results of the previous November. The assignment may qualify as the most pedestrian of the legislative year.

As Speaker Stephan Morse announced the names, one in particular got the members' attention.

"The member from Bennington, Mr. Wright." the Speaker announced.

The acoustic perfection of the House Chamber amplified the full fury of the Wrightian response: "Why that wimp! He sends [Rep.] DeBonis to Puerto Rico [to a legislative conference] and me to Room 11 to count votes."

The Speaker, with a rising reddening complexion, reached for a sheaf of papers under his lectern and, to my dismay, emphatically penciled out one line. Immediately after adjournment, I rushed to his office.

"I know what you did but I really got to have Ralph on my Committee! I really need him!" There was, without question, an unseemly tinge of desperation to my plea.

"He's going to Fish and Game," the feared purgatory of legislative banishment.

After a second effort of verbal prostration, there was a glint of moderation.

"Can you control him?"

"Yes," I said.

It was the worst exaggeration of my abilities in my entire legislative career. Ralph Wright was the most skillful politician I met in my years in the legislature. He not only imported his South Boston educational skills to Vermont, but he filled his own "legislative information trove" with a separate mental file folder for each member of the House. This "file" not only identified biographical detail, but listed strengths, weakness, and, occasionally, a tidbit or two of a few nocturnal activities that would not be included in a member's official biography.

Ralph and I shared not only a friendship, but similar public policy sentiments that fused the blue collar values of South Boston with those of an immigrant upbringing. The question was simple: is this going to help low income children, oldsters living on social security, or the folks who carry a lunch pail to work every day?

Ralph not only was a superb counter of votes to construct a legislative majority, but he left little to the greater (and uncontrollable) uncertainties of chance. In advance of each legislative biennium, before the election campaign began, Ralph met with every Democratic candidate in the hopeful's home district. He had recruited many personally. He dispensed campaign advice, a near religious zest for the holiness of the mission, and, on some occasions, an envelope containing a modest campaign offering if he thought this was a necessary lubricant for an election night victory. These political strategy sessions included a few carefully selected Republicans who had not only personal reasons for spurning their party's Speaker choice, but were not unmindful of a sought-after committee assignment the new Speaker could dispense. On the first day of the new legislative session those honored could express their gratitude with a simple X in the secret ballot election of the Speaker of the House.

That courting and wooing ritual, in 1984, elected Ralph Wright Speaker even though final election night tabulations showed Democrats at the minority end of the vote split. At least four nominal members of the opposing fraternity were persuaded to help forge a hold-your-breath 76 to 74 victory. It was the first of five such leadership elections that made Ralph Wright, my friend and fellow immigrant (from Dorchester), the longest serving Speaker of the Vermont House of Representatives.

In the pre-Wright era, in my early years in the House, there was a partnering that leaped over party label barriers. When an issue of importance was on the House floor, an informal team of committee chairpersons from both parties would rise and speak to help nudge the proposal toward a majority. This climate was nurtured by the first, the very first, Democrat Speaker of the House, Timothy O'Connor of Brattleboro. He was careful to appoint committee chairpersons more by the yardstick of ability rather than on the scale of party affiliation. It produced a near even split among both Republicans and Democrats.

More important to me, he had no qualms about parceling out leadership positions to the sibling team in the House—one as head of Health and Welfare and the other as Chairwoman of the Appropriations Committee. However, there was no doubt about the pecking order. The brother was the junior member on the scale of influence. The House rules said so.

They required that whenever the Health and Welfare Committee passed any bill that involved money, it had to go first to the Appropriations Committee, before it could be considered by the entire House. I had to testify before my sister's committee before the legislative gate could be raised. There usually was an expanded press corps with one sibling in the witness chair and the other holding her presiding baton.

Madeleine, Edgar, Arthur and Judith celebrating, 1985.

It was an affectionate competition. Neither of us ever shed the star-dusted marvel at the opportunity given us by our adopted country and, most generously, by the citizens of one of its smallest states. A few years later, this was part of the emotional swirl on the morning the Speaker of the House appointed me to escort my sister into the chamber to be sworn in as the first woman governor of Vermont.

As we waited outside the great mahogany doors for the Sergeant-at-Arms to announce the new governor, there was a grainy picture in my head, a flickering frame from the past: The two of us, standing on the fog-shrouded deck of an ocean liner... a mother's voice saying... it was important to be dressed and on deck on the morning we're coming to America.

"Mr. Speaker," the Sergeant-at-Arms shouted, "The Honorable Madeleine May Kunin, Governor-elect."

Our arms entwined, we walked down the carpeted aisle. Madeleine was radiant, in a tailored white suit, waving as she acknowledged the bi-partisan cheers of Representatives and Senators amid the standing-room-only crowd of guests.

A few hours later, the Senate named me chairman of its Appropriations Committee. The sibling shadow hovered nearby. The newly minted governor, with a retinue of press in tow, swept by as I was standing in the doorway of my new Committee room. She stopped to give me a hug and announced in the loudest whisper I ever heard:

"Congratulations!" she said. Accompanied by a cat-that-swallowed-the-canary smile, she added a postscript, "I'm not going to tell them you flunked math."

Within an hour after she was sworn in, the new governor moved into her suite on the top floor of the Executive Office Building. She inspected her new, ample quarters, including the governor's private bathroom, discreetly located behind an oak door. The previous occupant had left the toilet seat in its time-honored, male position: vertical. Unrecorded in the annals of Vermont history was the first unofficial act of the new governor. Governor Kunin lowered that seat to horizontal where it would comfortably rest for the next six years.

Governor Kunin and Senator May, in the executive offices, 1985.

With Peter and Lisa Kunin, early 1990s.

Edgar and Judith with Ambassador Madeleine Kunin, and three of her children—Peter, Julia and Adam—at swearing-in ceremony at the State Department, 1996.

Daniel Kunin and Edgar, 1997.

Julia Kunin and Edgar in 2009.

Learning pastry-making at the New England Culinary Institute, shortly after retiring from the Senate, 1991.

CHAPTER TWELVE

Legislature 3

A tribe of lawmakers is a community of its own. It harbors a unique village. It is a political village in a maelstrom of conflicting opinions, occasionally dramatized by a member's thespian-fueled temper tantrum. It is a spectator sport not only for those in the visitors' gallery but also for those in the House Chamber.

On a particularly frigid Vermont morning, the gray shrouded winter chill sometimes is contrasted by the warming—occasionally heated—speechifying of this obstreperous, eccentric band of fragile and enlarged egos. This unique tribe may include an uncle or maybe a cousin, who you might be embarrassed to claim as kinfolk, yet feel obliged to invite to Thanksgiving dinner. As a diverse group, the Vermont Legislature is a rural flavored mosaic of democracy. It is a micro community mirroring a macro community of independent souls who almost always place personal friendships above partisan politics, but have enough Yankee pragmatism not to let one color the other when it comes time to vote.

The Vermont Legislature, in the galaxy of American politics, had been an enduring Republican star that had contained the comfort of consistency—nearly a hundred years of it—until it was jolted in the 1936 Presidential election when the Green Mountain State achieved a modicum of notoriety because a bit of cherished political faith crumbled: "As Maine goes, so goes the nation." The time-honored prophesy of national election forecasters abruptly was demolished. That year it was revised by a tart tongued observer: "As Maine goes, so goes Vermont." The two Republican bastions were the only states that refused to give their electoral votes to President Franklin Delano Roosevelt.

In more recent times Vermont's political coloring has done a rainbow transformation from near solid Republican red to emphatic blue. In the Senate, at the end of the first decade of the new century, the ever shrinking Republican banner flew over only seven of the 30 polished mahogany desks in its ornate chamber. The Grand Old Party was so undernourished that there were not enough troops to put at least one Republican on each of the ten legislative committees. The Democrat/Republican split was 23 Democrats to 7 Republicans. Thirty-six years earlier, the numbers were similar except for one thing—they were exactly reversed.

In the new millennium the House of Representatives has mirrored this transformation. The sparse band of Republican souls occupied less than a third of the 150 member chamber that had been ruled by a seemingly hereditary gavel held by an uninterrupted phalanx of Republican Speakers. This stunning shift in political allegiance saw increasing numbers of Vermonters admit—in public—that they actually were Democrats.

The new majority had become so numerous that it was no longer political sport to engage in partisan jousting with so few on the other side. Instead, the political adrenalin of the Democrats sometimes was more enthusiastically aimed at one another.

On the Senate floor, 1986.

The change from Yankee caution and conservatism to a more liberal public policy agenda began when I was a member of the House and escalated in the years I was in the Senate. Occasionally it was an eyebrow raising jolt. The new devil-may-care spirit of Democrats was trumpeted at their 1988 Democratic State Convention. The rambunctious faithful nominated the Rev. Jesse Jackson as the Presidential candidate over their neighboring Massachusetts Governor Michael Dukakis, the party's eventual nominee.

This new political fault line was also affected by a previous major ballot change that permanently helped alter the results of Vermont elections. It was a seismic shift that put the spotlight on the individual candidate instead of the political party. Ever since anybody could remember, the ballot had included two big circles at the top of the two columns of candidates—the column of Republicans, on the left where the eye would focus first, and a second column on the right, listing the Democrats. An "X" in either of the big circles at the top meant you voted for all the brethren listed below, from governor to your local constable, although voters could still split their tickets.

The new ballot abolished the one "X" fits all option. It first listed each political aspirant's name. The candidate's political pedigree came *after* the name. Voters had to focus on the individual before knowing anything about party allegiance. The law altered Vermont elections and, incidentally, split the sibling legislative duet. Again, the issue was less philosophical than pragmatic. It was a contest between the few places in Vermont that barely could call themselves cities and the folks in the countryside.

In Madeleine's urban Burlington district, with its hefty Democrat majority, many were content with the old ways. Put an "X" in the big circle and you anointed the entire slate. In my district once you saw the Republican column, you had to split your vote if you wanted to vote for a Democrat like me. When you had to focus on the name and not the party, the contest became a choice among individuals and not of political labels.

Two elections later, I was convinced the new ballot was the difference that elected my sister governor in an extremely tight outcome that was not decided until the morning of the next day. The victory margin had edged to 3,700 votes out of 173,000 cast. Vermont had elected its first ever woman governor. Without the new ballot and with Ronald Reagan at the top of the Republican list, the impulse to vote a straight party ticket would have been compelling.

The influx of new Vermonters and the revised ballot were not the only reasons for Vermont's transformation from conservative orthodoxy to one of the most liberal states in the nation. Political and cultural changes were multiple. They were both ideological and physical.

Among the key changes that fundamentally altered both the culture and especially the voters of Vermont was a major national initiative. The construction of an Interstate Highway System changed America and, particularly, Vermont. The incessant clatter of the bulldozer's treads not only telescoped distances, but was the harbinger of unprecedented development. The polished and worn blades scraped away the last barriers of the previously isolated rural landscape. The new Interstate transformed Vermont and created a second economy. A large tourist economy that opened the land to a new migration of second home owners, weekend refugees fleeing a cacophony of car honking discord amid the clutter of bumper-to-bumper tensions of the city. The Vermont Development Department's slogan, "VERMONT, The Beckoning Country" fell on receptive urban ears. And an increasing number of "the new people" decided just a weekend escape was not enough. They packed their newly ordered L.L. Bean flannel shirts and became latter day frontiersmen in their new country outposts.

The urban immigrants not only populated the land, they imported different values and aspirations that soon showed up in Vermont's citizen legislature. The comfort that Vermont public policy making would be in the hands of common sense, generation-rooted natives became just one more vanishing touchstone. Their legislative dominance disappeared. At the dawn of the 21st century, less than a third of the Senate chamber's members could claim the "born-right-here" label.

In the House of Representatives those who had to confess migrating from "A-way" also saw their numbers rise dramatically. Furthermore, in a state that is one of the most rural in the nation, less than a handful of farmers are now in either chamber.

Are there so few farmers in the contemporary legislature because they no longer want to serve or because now they can't go home when it's time to start the spring ritual of sugaring or get started plowing their fields? In earlier decades, everybody went home when the sap started flowing. The commitment of a citizen legislator used to end in time for March Town Meeting. In more recent times members congratulate themselves when they can go home before mid-May. The current complexity of issues and the time to consider them has challenged the legislature's legitimacy as a representative convention of Vermonters. Is it really a "citizens' legislature" when only a small minority of citizens can take more than five months off to serve in the State Capitol? I could not serve in today's legislature and meet the needs I had 35 years ago. I could not take off nearly half a year and ignore my regular bread and butter work. More important, my friend John Murphy, the member from Ludlow, the long serving Dean of the House, wouldn't be able to either. A machinist at a General Electric plant in his hometown, he barely could negotiate a three month leave of absence from his employer, but an absence of half the year? Unlikely.

Representative Murphy was far more than the most veteran member among us. He was the uncensored voice of Vermont working men and women, a squat, rotund dynamo whose blue collar intensity was not just around his neck, but spanned his entire geography, from the tip of his hair to his toenails. Whenever he was recognized by the Speaker, you knew you were about to hear the voice of the working folk, plain Anglo-Saxon that never left you confused about his point, or more likely, his target.

On a rare occasion, the feisty member from Ludlow could get entangled in the verbal thickets where enthusiasm overwhelmed details. In one such oration, reporting a bill for his General and Military Affairs Committee, he concluded his reportage with the assurance that he and his colleagues had endorsed the bill by a 9 to 2 vote. Speaker Wright gently reminded Murphy that he, as Speaker, had appointed only nine members to the General and Military Affairs Committee. Staring at the Speaker's podium, Murphy hesitated before forming an emerging sunrise smile, as he confessed to this reality. With a wave of the hand, he seamlessly shifted into a higher gear.

"Mr. Speaker, if I may?"

"Yes, Member from Ludlow?"

"You're right, Mr. Speaker." The confession was followed by a skilled thespian's pause before the member from Ludlow continued. "*If* I had eleven members on my committee," with a hand now reaching skyward for heavenly concurrence, "My guess is it would have been 9 to 2."

Sen. May near the Muckross Pond outlet, in Springfield.

Through the years John and I collaborated on efforts that ranged from raising the minimum wage (consistently higher than the low ball federal minimum) to an eleventh hour land purchase, snatching a lake shore property from developers.

We turned a former Boy Scout camp into a state park that provided the only public swimming and picnic area at one of the larger lakes in southern Vermont. It didn't hurt that the land was in Murphy's district and the money was in my Appropriations Committee.

John always patiently listened to my suggestion for a partnership.

"May, that's alright," he would respond with a confirming nod punctuating the sentence. "That'll wake 'em up."

John Francis Murphy died November 9, 2011, mourned by his political adversaries and his supporters alike. The Annunciation of the Blessed Virgin Catholic Church in Ludlow was packed. Speaker Ralph Wright came from his retirement home in Florida to deliver the eulogy, the final heartfelt gift of one Irishman to another.

Among the litany of modern challenges to the citizen legislature there is one important cohort that has expanded rather than contracted in its climb to greater equality. The once virtually all-male club has been dismantled. In my freshman year there was a lone woman senator among her 29 business-suited, neck-tied, aftershave-scented colleagues. Since then, women senators have increased tenfold. In the House female legislators more than doubled from 20 to 57. They now represent more than a third of its members.

The warmth I feel about the fading rituals may camouflage the complexity of today's public policy arena. Our on-a-first-name greeting in our micro society, the smell of wood smoke carried on the autumn wind, the pot-luck lunch break of March Town Meeting are among those warm memories for me. Yet even the sap buckets hanging from maple trees have succumbed to technology creep. The photographer's scene of wooden buckets on a tree-lined country road has been replaced by a grid of plastic tubing, looping from tree to tree with the sap flowing to the large, metal storage tank next to the sugar house. The wooden buckets are now most likely found only on tourist-bound syrup cans with their painted portrait of nostalgia: a team of horses pulling the sap-gathering sleigh across hummocks of melting snow. The contemporary citizen legislature, like the artist's team, may be stabled more in the warmth of recollection than in reality.

In the past half century the Vermont Legislature has changed more dramatically than at any time since Ira Allen, Ethan's brother, certified Vermont's own Declaration of Independence when he was clerk of the state's 1777 Convention. The teeter-totter of political power that teetered in only one direction—Republican—has been dramatically reversed. The dominating mix of "born right here" Vermonters has shifted to those of us who migrated from elsewhere. The pool of citizens who can serve in what has become a close to six month job has vastly diminished. Most Vermonters have to earn a living with more substantial financial rewards than the modest salary paid only when the legislature actually is in session. The problem was illustrated by Speaker Ralph Wright's pay check. Every week it contained fewer dollars than that of his secretary.

The fundamental changes among those shaping the state's public policy priorities have become a national dilemma, drifting far beyond the mountains of Vermont. They are pushing the last remaining citizen legislatures into the red Danger

Zone. They are eroding the essential support beams of "down home" democracy. The size of the state and the composition of its legislature is not a factor. The information explosion and its flood of special interest money have produced a Niagara of facts, and sometimes artfully constructed fiction masquerading as facts. Not since Gutenberg created movable type has mass information expanded at such a torrid pace.

In a small state like Vermont, yet to reach the population of a mid-size American city, the information tide is so massive it collides with "that-can't-be-right" disbelief. In a recent year the e-mails sent to legislators swamped the State House. Seventeen million separate messages were directed at 150 Representatives and 30 Senators. In one recent January, the e-mail avalanche multiplied from 283,322 to 1,129,830 over the previous January.

This information onslaught required the legislative Council to hire a contractor just to screen the overload. Nearly 96% were blocked, sent to the electronic waste basket because they were irrelevant. Even with 4% that passed muster, the average legislator received about ten e-mails every day whether the legislature was in session or not. In contrast, 40 years earlier during my freshman year I might have received a half-dozen letters during the week from people in my district. This meant a hot-under-the-collar issue was brewing.

Beyond the modern barrage of information—most of it useless, dispatched to the junk mailbox—is the contemporary complexity of controversial issues and the growth of legislative proposals to fix them. In some years the quantity of these bills nearly tripled while those surviving the process dwindled to a fraction.

In the mid-1990s, 517 bills were introduced in the biennium. More than two-thirds became law. In the past few years the number of bills proposed nearly tripled to a one year high of 1,420. A scant 15% survived the journey from the House, through the Senate, to the governor for the signing ceremony.

Beyond the time requirements to serve and the skimpy compensation, there is the premiere hobgoblin of American politics: money. Ever cascading amounts of it. Fund raising sometimes competes with the debate of new ideas or the reevaluating of old ones, the very purpose of the place. Too often the frenzied search for campaign dollars has become the dominant currency of the public square. It might not replace votes, but it helps produce them. More important, this gold rush quest for dollars significantly limits the field of candidates.

Even in Vermont, a miniature stage of American politics, a campaign for a two-year term for governor now requires more than a million dollars. How many can raise that money? More importantly, raise it without making promises that begin to encroach on moral boundaries?

The financial requirements for political campaigns have been upended. The changes are startling. The 1948 expenditure report filed by one of Vermont's most admired U.S. Senators, George Aiken, appears now like imaginings plucked from a Victorian political novel. He spent $124 on a statewide United States Senate campaign. Senator Patrick Leahy, the current long-time incumbent, in his most recent re-election effort, began with a campaign bundle of $5.2 million.

In my last Vermont Senate campaign report in 1990, my expenses totaled $3,232. None of these dollars were spent on radio, television or newspaper advertising. The majority was paid at the gas pump for my nightly travels across my huge senatorial district.

This new litany of complexity—particularly the cascade of money, the proliferation of special interest voices, the increased time demands of sorting contentious public issues— has combined to erode the citizen legislature. Every once in a while, however, this erosion is stopped because of the emotional tensions of a particular dramatic issue. It anchors the one quality a free, self-governing society cannot do without: personal courage.

I was no longer in the legislature when civil unions between same sex couples roiled Vermonters like no other public issue in decades, if ever. The political lives of some of those who faced the "Yes" or "No" roll call could be determined by this single vote. On the Lilliputian political scene of Vermont the legislators are not a formless, nameless pejorative. More often they are faces most Vermonters recognize. They might have seen them that week at the general store, or sat next to them at Saturday's high school football game. They are often neighbors.

This proximity made the debate on civil unions an especially painful choice. This was particularly challenging in the "Kingdom," Vermont's most northern outpost that fused its isolation with generations-cherished independence. The traditions were hand-me-down values. They were fixed, as certain as anything could get, fortified by such customs of permanence like attending church on Sunday and bringing a covered dish to the community dinner.

It was a comfort, as reassuring as the certitude that comes with the change of seasons, as repetitive as the fall ritual of preserving the garden's summer bounty in the steam-sealed canning jars that would be stored in a dark corner in the root cellar. They were hereditary values. They expected the folks they sent to the legislature to honor them.

In this cultural and political congregation was Representative Robert Kinsey, a dairy farmer from Craftsbury Common, a hamlet of about 940 people in the northeast hard-scrabble corner of the state, just 35 miles from the Canadian border. Rep. Kinsey was an unlikely "Yes" vote for same sex couples.

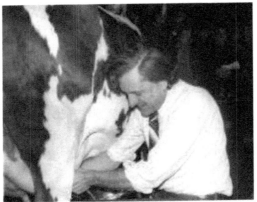

Edgar competing in the legislative milking contest.

He and I, on more than a few occasions, were on opposite sides of a roll call. But we had a common bond, cows, and their at least twice-a-day habit of needing to be milked. We both grew up on a dairy farm, and later became enthusiastic rivals in the annual legislative milking contest that pitted the House against the Senate at the annual State Farm Show.

Bob Kinsey was more than a farmer/legislator. For 30 years he represented his neighbors in the House of Representatives and for several years his Republican colleagues chose him as their leader. He had come one vote short of being elected Speaker. He and his wife sang in the chorus of the East Craftsbury Common Presbyterian church. They had bought their 347 acre farm at a Depression era price of $6,300, mostly with borrowed money.

Elections in Craftsbury were not imprisoned by the bitter rhetoric of contemporary political combat. They involved folks who knew each other, more often than not, liked each other. Bob Kinsey's consistent political opponent was Francis Whitcomb who had what was at the time a debilitating handicap. He had a (D) for *Democrat*, after his name. Every Sunday Bob and Francis Whitcomb stood next to each other, scanning the sheet music in the bass section of the East Craftsbury United Presbyterian church choir. They celebrated the "Lord's Day" together, blending their voices in praise of Him.

Both Bob and Eunice Kinsey knew about the joy and pain of a shared life. On one frost-etched November morning, Bob had dug a grave, by hand, on a rise above his farm house where he buried his son who had ended his life.

Rep. Kinsey could have been a prototype in a folktale about generations of toughened Vermont farmers whose calloused hands reflected the biography of earning a living from a hard-scrabble land. He might have been a nominee for the cover of the state's tourist promotion magazine. Until he voted for same sex civil unions.

Before that vote he had built a tepee as a warming hut next to his skating rink. He had built it for his family and his neighbors. The tepee mysteriously caught fire and burned to the ground. The fire theories were multiple. The fire chief thought it might have been chipmunks who dragged matches to the bottom of the stairs. The more cynical thought it was arson. That next summer 15 House members—Republicans and Democrats—came to Craftsbury Common to help him rebuild it. He also had rigged a generator at the rink so there would be some light for night time skating. The generator was stolen.

In the election after his civil union vote Bob was defeated in the Republican primary. He ran as an Independent in the general election. He lost. In the 2002 contest he switched parties and ran as a Democrat. His neighbors rejected him again. David Moats, the editorial page editor of *The Rutland Herald* who won a Pulitzer Prize for his editorials about the civil union debate's searing mixture of love and hate, may have captured the essence of Robert Kinsey in three simple sentences:

> He and his wife, Eunice, had attended the same Presbyterian Church for more than fifty years. They had learned something about life and love and death. No one was going to instruct him about right and wrong or the disposition of his soul.

Robert Kinsey, for me, was another kind of prototype. He had become a symbol for the one quality a free, self-governing society cannot do without. The personal courage of those on this sometimes fractious stage. He was not alone. Sixteen legislators who answered the Civil Unions roll call with a "Yes" vote were defeated in the next election. Among them was a retired State Trooper who for decades enforced Vermont laws as he swore to do when he first took his oath of office. Now, suddenly, he was confronted by a potential law that approved same sex unions. He voted "Yes."

The list included a housewife who the previous Sunday had heard her priest rail against civil unions. In spite of the sermon, she voted "Yes." Their answer was not just a moral choice, but harbored an understanding that the response could be career ending. Suddenly that simple word—courage—had become the north star of Vermont politics.

The fevered controversy brought legislators together who rarely voted with each other. Representative John Francis Murphy and Representative Robert Everett Kinsey were not only geographically separated, but their political convictions were often as distant as their districts—southern Vermont and the Northeast Kingdom. But they came together, bonding, on a public policy pinnacle where the "Yes" or "No" answer is distilled into a purely moral question and no longer is just a discomforting political quandary. Neither man's colleagues expected them to answer "Yes" to this historic roll call.

"Mr. Speaker," Rep. Murphy began, on the day of the vote. "As I listened today I have searched my soul and found that I've been wrong..." This was the introduction to the member from Ludlow's confession. It reverberated through a you-could-hear-a-pin drop silence in the House of Representatives.

"In the past I have done everything I could to kill the gay rights bill. In the past I've been on the wrong side, Mr. Speaker. I've changed my mind. Today I hope to do what is right. I'm going to support this bill. I can assure my colleagues this bill isn't any different than those that I helped to kill in the past. It's me, Murphy, who's different."

This speech, more than any other in his 30 year legislative career, explained who Rep. Murphy really was. It became the capstone of remembrance in Ralph Wright's eulogy. Speaker Wright described his friend's confession. "The entire House sat in stunned silence," Speaker Wright recalled. "And then like a summer cloud burst came a thunder of applause unlike any I had ever experienced in the House."

I never had the chance to discuss John Murphy's or Robert Kinsey's vote with them. I don't presume to know the emotional turmoil that formed their response. I suspect Bob Kinsey understood the consequences of this vote. It could be career ending. He knew that his neighbors could punish him.

I was no longer emotionally involved. Like other Vermonters, I was a spectator. I had retired from the Senate long before gay marriage appeared on the political horizon. But I knew that these moments are as exhilarating as they are emotionally difficult—palm sweating difficult. In my 16 years in the political arena, they stand out like no others.

Such policy debates are listed in the course catalogue of academia under "Political Science." But they are not a science at all. They are, instead, an emotional, personal intersection that demands a moral accounting in the bookkeeping of your soul.

These are the decisions you remember because they make you reach deep inside of yourself. They make you examine your core values, probing, questioning—what do you really believe? They are emotional dramas that are thrust on the center stage of public debate. It seems that everybody is watching. Each spectator is incubating an emotional, personal opinion—very personal—about the headline-making issue: a vote on abortion, a roll call about the death penalty, and, maybe the catapult to a personal political obituary wrapped in a "Yes" response to gay marriage.

It is an arena where we all have had early training. We have been challenged, prodded by the discomforting simplicity of that choice. In our growing up years we have been tested.

In the fourth grade, if I don't know the answer during the weekly quiz, do I peek at the test paper on my neighbor's desk when the teacher has her back turned?

As a teenager when I pay for the candy bar and soda, and clerk hands me too much change, do I return the extra coins?

These are the private choices that rattle around the hallways of our conscience. They are individual, uncomfortable maybe, but insulated from public view, intensely our own. But for every public official these choices are instantly exposed, explosively public.

The clerk of the House of Representatives calls my name. He waits for my answer. "Yes" or "No." There is no room for a compromise offer. No space for speeches, qualifiers, explanations. No terrycloth bathrobe to hide my nakedness.

"The member from Springfield, Mr. May?"

The clerk's pen hovers over his tally sheet. He waits. The legislators around me are looking in my direction. There is a momentary blank space. I answer.

A few hours later my vote is on that night's television news. The next morning it appears in the black and white clarity of the roll call listing in the newspaper. Everybody knows.

It is the summit of personal discomfort, the terrain where fear grapples with morality in full public view. It is the oldest struggle of human kind: choosing between right and wrong.

Samuel Kunin with his great-uncle Edgar, 2006.

Edgar with grand-nephew, Jacob Kunin, at the Recreation Center he helped found in Springfield, Vt., about 2008.

Edgar May won a Pulitzer Prize for local reporting for a series on the troubled welfare system in 1961, while a reporter at *The Buffalo Evening News.* He is the author of <u>The Wasted Americans</u> and numerous articles on America's prison system and other social reforms.

He was a reporter for several newspapers, including Vermont weeklies, the *Chicago Tribune,* and the *Fitchburg* (Mass) *Sentinel.*

He served in the Vermont House of Representatives from Springfield, 1974–82 where he chaired the Health and Welfare committee. He served in the Vermont Senate from Windsor County, 1984–1990, and was appointed to the Senate Appropriations committee. He served sixteen years in the Vermont State House, before he retired in 1991. He was a politician in the best sense: dedicated to improving the lives of others, especially the most vulnerable.

Prior to his Vermont career, May served in the federal government as a Special Assistant to Sargent Shriver, the first director of the Peace Corps. He became Deputy Director of the domestic Peace Corps, VISTA. May was a Foreign Service officer in France while he worked with Sargent Shriver, his long time friend and mentor.

President Lyndon Johnson asked him to come to Washington to work on the War on Poverty, as a result of The Wasted Americans. He became Inspector of the War on Poverty office of Economic Opportunity.

After his political career, May worked as COO of Special Olympics International in Washington with Eunice Shriver, 1993–1995.

He has served on many boards, including the University of Vermont, the Vermont Symphony Orchestra, and the Vermont Student Assistance Corporation. In 2004 he was named Citizen of the Year by the regional Chamber of Commerce.

Throughout his life, May was dedicated to public service. He was inspired to better the lives of both the youth and the elderly citizens of Springfield, Vermont. The construction of the Edgar May Recreational Center was the culmination of his efforts and would not have come about without him.

Edgar May was born in Zurich, Switzerland in 1929. His mother, Renée May, brought him and his sister, Madeleine Kunin, to the United States at the outbreak of World War II in 1940. He attended Columbia University School of General Studies and graduated from Medill School of Journalism at Northwestern University, summa cum laude. He was inducted into the school's Hall of Achievement in 1997.